Aquarius

How to Seduce and Date the Aquarius Man

(Understanding Your Own Innate Aquarius Personality Traits)

Jeffrey Lippert

Published By **Bella Frost**

Jeffrey Lippert

All Rights Reserved

Aquarius: How to Seduce and Date the Aquarius Man (Understanding Your Own Innate Aquarius Personality Traits)

ISBN 978-1-77485-782-3

No part of this guidebook shall be reproduced in any form without permission in writing from the publisher except in the case of brief quotations embodied in critical articles or reviews.

Legal & Disclaimer

The information contained in this ebook is not designed to replace or take the place of any form of medicine or professional medical advice. The information in this ebook has been provided for educational & entertainment purposes only.

The information contained in this book has been compiled from sources deemed reliable, and it is accurate to the best of the Author's knowledge; however, the Author cannot guarantee its accuracy and validity and cannot be held liable for any errors or omissions. Changes are periodically made to this book. You must consult your doctor or get professional medical advice before using any of the suggested remedies, techniques, or information in this book.

Upon using the information contained in this book, you agree to hold harmless the Author from and against any damages, costs, and expenses, including any legal fees potentially resulting from the application of any of the information provided by this guide. This disclaimer applies to any damages or injury caused by the use and application, whether directly or indirectly, of any advice or information presented, whether for breach of contract, tort, negligence, personal injury, criminal intent, or under any other cause of action.

You agree to accept all risks of using the information presented inside this book. You need to consult a professional medical practitioner in order to ensure you are both able and healthy enough to participate in this program.

Table Of Contents

Introduction _____ 1

Chapter 1: Horoscope 2021 Aquarius According To The Year Of Birth _____ 4

Chapter 2: Horoscope For Winter Of 2021. Aquarius _____ 14

Chapter 3: Horoscope 2021 Aquarius By The Year Of Birth _____ 26

Chapter 4: Horoscope For January 2021 Aquarius _____ 37

Chapter 5: Horoscope For The Month Of March 2021 Aquarius _____ 54

Chapter 6: Horoscope For April 2021 Aquarius 63

Chapter 7: The Fixed Sign Characteristics Of The Aquarians _____ 72

Chapter 8: Aquarius Personality _____ 94

Chapter 9: Aquarius Friendship _____ 131

Chapter 10: The Big Picture _____ 170

Conclusion _____ 184

Introduction

Aquarius The eleventh sign in the zodiac is the symbol for the water bearer. It is fixed as well as an airy one. It is an ominous sign that is which is ruled by planet SATURN. These four characteristics are what make the person born in Aquarius different from the other. The characteristics of Saturn and the fixed and stable character of the sign together with the air quality, i.e. swiftly moving with the speed of wind , made it difficult for anyone to know their individuality even if they're not involved in Astrology. They appear mysterious to a lot of their closest relatives. In order to comprehend the characteristics of the Aquarius person, we first must understand the origins and the nature of the sign Aquarius.

The Aquarius people, whether by the sun sign (Western Astrology) or by moon sign (Eastern Astrology) or born within that ascendant will exhibit these traits as well as the common.

In the beginning, we can determine which people are Aquarians

As per the Sun sign

If you were born during the time period from January 20th through February 19th of any year in which you are born, and the SUN is in the zone of the zodiac, you belong to the Aquarius sign of western astrology.

Based on the moon's sign

If you were born under the signification of KUMBHA (which is the name used in the eastern astrology) or if you have your birthplace within any of the mentioned constellations. Dhanista-3, 4 padas, Sathabhisham - 1, 2, 3, 4 padas, Poorvabhadra - 1, 2, 3, padas.

In accordance with the ascendant

If your birth occurs when the sun is rising in this sign of the horizon then you're an Aquarius ascendant.

Of course , the characteristics aren't the same, but however, they all share the fundamental characteristics that make up an Aquarius.

The sun represents the soul, the Moon is the symbol of the mind and the Ascendant symbolizes physical nature. Therefore, regardless of whether they are a moon sign Aquarius or a zodiac symbol of Aquarius or are born into the ascendant the are Aquarians showing their qualities through their soul's nature or through their way of thinking, or their appearance or traits of personality.

Chapter 1: Horoscope 2021 Aquarius According To The Year Of Birth

The 2021 horoscope promises to Aquarius an extremely happy and prosperous time in every way. The roads will be wide for innovation, technical endeavor and growth in your career. But the energy source must be properly managed so that it doesn't lose focus and determination in the pursuit of objectives. Making new connections and establishing relationships with people who are like-minded are essential to the success.

Many of the wishes of Aquarius during this year, the Year of Metal Ox will come true. The recognition and fame will arrive simultaneously that could cause you to rethink your priorities. People who have dreamed of obtaining an executive position will be in a position of honor. But it is important to remember about decency and responsibility. In 2021, be prepared to compromise even when you are tempted to shout or slapping your business associate. Do not do that and show the power of diplomatic skills.

On the other side, Jupiter inspires Aquarius for transformation and transformation. On the other hand, Saturn and Uranus both restrain urges, while the other is not pleased by sudden changes or events which thwart plans. Let go of stubbornness, accept things as it is, and let go of the circumstance. You'll benefit from the patience of a professional and thoughtful project planning.

The horoscope for 2021 suggests Aquarius to make their own decisions regarding personal issues. It could be a trade, business or creative activities. If you have faith in everyone who you collaborate with and you trust them, it can lead to successful. The ability to make independent decisions is also a good thing however only in specific situations. For instance in a relationship, try to achieve more fidelity than freedom. Have you walked before.

When it's the Year of the Ox, the most bizarre scenarios can be a possibility when communication with others. If you're confident about your achievements and achievements, people will be hesitant to talk to them. Be honest and genuine in your friendship Be more modest. In intimate relationships, Aquarius should be more flexible and sensitive. Unfortunately adhering to the rules is not the best way to go.

Horoscope 2021 advises Aquarius to steer toward creation, but not destroy all that he has constructed. Aversion and envy aren't the ideal companions to the workplace. Particularly if you were involved in initiatives with new colleagues. Avoid showing too much the qualities of a leader, instead, you should be more wise and more sane. For financial matters in this Year of the Ox, honesty must be the top priority. Through deceitful methods it is impossible to be able to get what you want.

The mystical and the mysterious aren't your forte in this year's White Bull. If Aquarius is suspicious, or, to the contrary assertive in communicating, then he's likely to end up committing suicide using his own stylish "weapon". Be positive and you will be able to tackle problems you've dealt with multiple times.

2021 Aquarius man horoscopes for 2021

A vast array of exciting ideas are awaiting Aquarius men during The year of the Ox. Most important is that every idea is documented, not simply floating around out in the air. Make sure to implement them within the timeframe, and don't let the chance pass you by to get up and grab luck at the tail.

Horoscope 2021 of the Aquarius man will predict success in the social and professional arenas. Even rivals will retreat when they see your determination and vast experiences. It is your right to explore your boundaries, build strong contacts , and boost your standing.

A fantastic time for Aquarius males and women, who will equip themselves with a robust rear from January through July 2021. Don't look back at past failures, you deserve more. The ladder to success isn't as steep when you put your learning into action.

Aquarlus Woman 2021 Horoscope

The 2021 horoscope of the Aquarius woman is promising the possibility of success in a variety of directions. Your personal life will change as you become more assertive and confident in yourself. You'll be confident about the progress you are making in your work. If you are able to distribute your desires and strengths correctly the way you want to, you'll be on your way to health and happiness without any obstacles. Make sure you don't overdo the work during this Year of the Ox, relax more and save energy.

In July 2021 In July 2021, single Aquarius women are able to meet their "soul soul mate". It's possible that the man was already present in your life and you just didn't pay any focus. Consider a closer look at your new partner, and of them, there are worthy and trustworthy people.

The year's beginning in the year of White Bull will turn out to be extremely brilliant and decisive. Every idea and endeavor is bound to be successful, so stand firm on your feet.

Horoscope 2021 Aquarius significant aspects of your life

The 2021 Horoscope predicts the coming year to be a turbulent and challenging time for Aquarius. We'll need to be able to differentiate between our energy and our time to avoid be splintered into multiple pieces. Families, home, kids and a time with friends constant whirlwind and bustle. There is no way to live without moral support and a community of like-minded individuals when you are working in the year of the Ox. But don't count solely on your family and friends. Be sure not to do something wrong!

The most important thing to remember in 2021 is to not look in the past. It's here - the present and the present take a deep breath! Aquarius requires something they enjoy so that they can be occupied not just their hands but also thoughts. Don't forget your talents and desires and you shouldn't be acting solely for the sake of others. You should try to be entangled by something new and exciting, while keeping your mind from the everyday routine.

Aquarius 2021 horoscope advises to reduce friendships. It's possible that with someone you're no longer in contact The difference in opinions about things can be felt. Read a good book or watching a movie that is meaningful or just being in the company of the natural world. This year, in the year of

White Bull, sports will be a great method to boost your immunity. Take note of your appearance as well as delicious food and also the sexual aspect of your life. All that can bring you joy is amazing. However, don't overdo it as they could lead you to a wrong or dangerous road.

The physical state of Aquarius in 2021 won't disappoint you. You're full of strength as well as energy. Most importantly, you should not neglect activities that are active. Be in touch with your family members more frequently take note of their ideas and wishes.

Horoscope 2021 Aquarius A successful area of activity

This year, in the Year of The Metal Ox, Aquarius needs to concentrate first on their own personal development, then take a look at public affairs. You must make some changes in your appearance, modify the fashion of clothes eliminate unhealthy habits, and enhance your overall health.

Horoscope 2021 Aquarius recommends being optimistic to overcome every obstacle in the path of life. You must be honest, noble and pleasant when dealing with others. If you wish to keep a your good name, be careful not to fall into a trap of adventure or deceit. The end result of working hard on yourself will not be to put yourself in a position to wait all day. In the year of the Ox, wonderful people will gravitate to you. You will be unique in judgement and fascinating in appearance.

A lot of people will seek out Aquarius in 2021 for guidance. It is not a good idea to ignore Aquarius as this can create energy to your work and confidence regarding personal issues. It is crucial not to get proud, and to not ignore the situation. Make your own promises and promises more seriouslyand make sure you keep your commitments on time.

The 2021 horoscope advises Aquarius to look at his self from every angle. If your figure isn't identical, then you should lose weight and exercise. Don't expect everything to get back to normal. Instead and take charge about your look. It's beneficial to upgrade your look, go to an expert stylist and beauty salon. Women with this type of sign should not be concerned with a fresh haircut and acquiring anti-aging skin products.

If you are born in the Year of the Ox it is possible to have the possibility to be in the ranks, find your life partner and improve your health. If Aquarius isn't a sloppy and "airy" the chances are that Aquarius will be able to get what that he desires. The most important thing is to establish achievable goals for you.

Horoscope 2021 Aquarius What to be concerned about

The horoscope 2021 tells Aquarius to be mindful not just of your own health, but also the health and wellbeing of your loved ones. Be more responsible and serious so as to not be rewarded with problems. Be sure to ask more often about what your family members and children do if you're an individual with a family. Quality is an option make use of it in debates and avoid conflicts. The year is White Bull, you will be working hard and be mindful about rest.

The family sector must be a top priority by 2021. However, it must be addressed with a focus on maintaining the culture of conduct and participation at the highest level in solving difficult problems.

What is the sense of living? Aquarius is often a reference to this question. This is not unusual, as people will often seek out new work, or study, and to improve their skills. Be confident and don't let yourself get bogged down and gain positive energy. It is beneficial to begin the path of wellness and transformation within yourself. Horoscope 2021 Aquarius doesn't recommend rebelling and relying solely on their own beliefs.

In the year of the Ox, there will be plenty of opportunities to rise up the ladder and undertake large projects. Your success will be based on whether you're a diligent worker and accurate in your business. Concentrate on the smallest tasksand they'll end up being economically beneficial. In the end, don't be apprehensive in 2021. Instead, make use of your reserves of energy wisely. Discipline and diligence are what will ensure the positive path of life. Sometimes, you require more effort to reach your goals than the ones you've established for yourself.

Chapter 2: Horoscope For Winter Of 2021. Aquarius

Horoscope 2021 Aquarius suggests focusing on your personal life during the winter months. If your family life has become dull and boring, it's all is yours to control. Particularly if issues in relationships with your spouse have arisen amid the backdrop of daily difficulties. Make a decision in advance and don't delay the repair or other matters. The intimacy of the Year of the Ox should be painted in romantic hues. But, it can't be without drama or conflict. Be able to control your urges become more soft and gentle.

Aquarius is unpredictable and windy by nature. This can adversely affect relationships with love. You might be wondering why you're yet to be lonely and haven't found a partner? It is obvious that you must modify or reconsider certain situations. It's an one thing to be carried by a person, it's quite another to love and cherish the person you love and respect. For the Winter of 2021 there's numerous opportunities to meet not just the "soul partner" and to make a happy and secure family.

A realistic perspective and a dose of optimism is is needed during 2021, which is the year of White Bull. If you don't have these traits and a sense of humor, you'll never be able to change in the direction that the horoscope of 2021 indicates for Aquarius. Display your talent, demonstrate your originality to the fullest and bring comfort to your family without fear or resentment.

A few Aquarius can rise up the career ladder. Strangely enough, winter is the best time for this, don't fall. But the changes may not just be pleasant, be prepared for the trials of the world. Conflicts with colleagues, conflicts between management and employees, as well as even job shifts are likely. The 19th of February is when finance will be the focus of your mind. Pay attention to the flow of money into your bank account. The most important thing is to not lose control and remain calm when doing things that can lead to your professional development.

This month, Aquarius can expect to see dramatic changes in personal and professional life. This time of year will be characterized by financial success and successes. Learn to be happy about small things, and don't rush to chase all the things. Check your health regularly, there could be a malfunction in the nervous system, or physical fatigue. If you have chronic illnesses and you want to treat them, you should focus on these. The effects will be evident by the close of winter 2021.

Spring horoscope 2021 Aquarius

The season of romance and love will begin with a beautiful start for Aquarius. However, the nature's unpredictable nature and the unpredictable nature of your behaviour can keep you in check. The relationship with the person you choose in 2021's spring is more like a storm, rather than a soft sea. The mood shifts, the demands to each other are made, and the passion is more than. We agree that it's impossible to be in the midst of such a tense time. Take things in an entirely different perspective, and do not be a burden to yourself and your spouse even if you don't already feel a connection.

The 2021 Horoscope predicts an uneasy end for Aquarius. It's more beneficial than living in deceit or "swimming" in the mud. After spring is over it is necessary to complete all the steps to begin free swimming. There is a chance that you'll find yourself in love with a person. It is said that you can't put your heart in a box.

March 2021 is a month that favors the finances of Aquarius It is possible that you'll discover hidden talents within you which could lead to opportunities for earning income. This is a great month for professions that require creativity. Between mid-April and May 2021 is a time that you can accumulate positive energy, discoveries, and unforgettable events for Aquarius. The ability to adapt and change your mind will be required in every endeavor that you do. Mercury is in Gemini will not let you go on your own, and will assist you to tackle any problem. It will require you work hard however, it will provide outstanding results in your career and financial planning.

The horoscope 2021 advises Aquarius to create a genuine change within him. Everyone is subject to external influences, but transforming spiritually is the primary goal. You're charismatic, distinct and gifted. You are destined to be the best and carving your place in the society. Jupiter is a major factor in the stability of your finances, and income will be a significant increase in the final days of spring.

March 2021 is an excellent time to lose weight and development of your physical. If excessive weight has resulted in some health issues take immediate action to begin an exercise program and eat a healthy diet. Aquarius must seek out a physician so as not to worsen the health condition.

Horoscope 2021 Aquarius recommends strengthening your immune system early in spring. Children are aware that hardening and vitamins can help them avoid colds. The weather can change drastically and can cause frequent bronchitis, runny nose and allergic reactions. It is important to stay clear of food items that could harm your hips, waist and hips. Are you looking to be more attractive? Chocolates, buns, and bacon smoked - off!

Summer horoscope 2021 Aquarius

At the end of summer 2021 Aquarius is going to feel at peace and content that he'll forget the previous hardships. It's great Keep it up! The most important thing is that the person who is hovering above the ground, inspired and accomplishment, is that it doesn't sink. The work, love and business realms are not affected by anything else that could already have positive effects on mood. As we enter the Year of the Ox, people can unwind completely, without having to interrupt work. It's surprising, but it's true. Aquarians will find something that is to their taste, and this can "feed" them through the close of August.

In terms of love, everything is going the right direction here. Horoscope 2021 Aquarius promises many meetings, novels and confessions. One person is expressing praises while another is taking a trip towards the Registry office. while the third is being ripped apart for the sake of pleasing you. Be cautious with your privacy. Work and health should not disappear into the background. This is particularly applicable to creative Aquarius. You may not feel the June energy, but do not get it back until the close of the year of the Ox.

In July, you'll be required to develop connections with your partners. Jupiter in Pisces is favorable to your earnings. When you reach the end of the month, you are able to close your professional projects and cases , and make your suitcases.

Aquarius during 2021's summer should not seek help from anyone. You have to take care of everything yourself, which will lead you to the point of success. Be aware that laziness and inaction can be a severe slap in the face. You could lose not just your reputation, but also everything you've built up through the years. Don't be a slave to routine and spontaneity follow a plan that is well-organized.

Aquarius 2021 horoscope advises you to be less dreamy and fly through the sky. It is important to be more practical and realistic to pay off any debts and take the right path.

You will face tests but they won't be too tough. Learn how to navigate between them, demonstrate the art of Reincarnation. Aquarius isn't likely to suffer from serious health issues during Aquarius's Year of the Ox. However, this doesn't mean you should abandon him. June 2021 is a fantastic time to run and train. The greens and vegetables are already maturing in the garden. Eat healthy and lose excess weight. In the midst of an stress the nervous system is likely to be affected. It is not necessary to go to doctors, but calm yourself internally, get more sleep and visit at the beaches during the weekend.

Horoscope for the autumn of 2021 Aquarius

If, from 2021's fall Aquarius is looking forward to something extraordinary and amazing, then it is it will be a waste of time. The time will be spent by Aquarius in his great work and vanity, as well as the search for new ideas. Family-wide change in the relationship with spouses aren't exempted. Unfortunately, they are they are not necessarily for the better. All the blame lies with jealousy, domestic breakdowns, and other such nonsense. Perhaps you and your partner, decide to quit traveling? Or perhaps you'd like to retire to an undiscovered village - complete with the help of a fishing rod and guitar?

Horoscope for 2021. Aquarius is not a good time to make loans or get money from your friends. Don't be too excited, the financial situation isn't that stressful. It is likely to be resolved in the event that you don't impose new obligations on you. You should work harder in the months of September and October as long as time and energy permit. If you've are considering changing careers or work location The future is now in their hands. All will be well!

Aquarius who are working on their work can sign agreements in this year's Year in the year of the Ox. Collaboration can prove very successful and beneficial financially. Be careful not to be too enthusiastic and impatient. Otherwise, you'll get caught up in showdowns and conflicts.

Competition will become fierce by the mid-autumn of 2021. If Aquarius isn't vigilant and precise in their proposals, they could impact their financial position severely. Make sure you weigh the advantages and disadvantages so as not to end up at risk of being in the red.

Aquarius 2021 horoscope advises against over-stimulation of the mind. The expression "all illnesses stem from the nerves" is not a flimsly in the making. You're not a machine that is constantly beat and slapped. Make sure you take care of yourself Do not work too much and take a break in the natural world. It's easy to breathe in the fall There are plenty of vitamins, and the urge to be creative will help you let go of everyday worries. The key is to delay treatment for ailments - both new and old ones during the Year of the Ox. In the event that you delay, the effects are serious.

What time to take a vacation in 2021? Aquarius

Horoscope 2021 Aquarius suggests writing an application to take a vacation in September. It is possible to arrange travel in any direction, and it is a great time. Furthermore, the job will not be huge, if you've finished everything in time. It's not a bad idea to purchase tickets to a destination in which you can take a break and soak up experiences. Excursions, meeting people, historical insights and a good night's rest All of this is going to be beneficial during the Year of the White Bull.

Strategies on Aquarius for 2021

In its nature Aquarius has a tendency to be chaotic and fluid, which can scare people away from Aquarius. In the beginning, they're amazed by the charismatic character but then they realize that friendship, and even an ongoing relationship is not going to work. Indeed, he is not averse to the monotony and routine is a burden on him. This is why problems occur at work, in the personal realm, and also in finance. This year, in the Year of the Ox it is recommended to make a change if you wish to have peace and stability of mind.

The horoscope for 2021 suggests that Aquarius frequently rely on his senses for clues. It's a unique sign for you. If you can use your third eye in various directions, you'll be able to stay clear of problems. Dream interpretation is more frequent They will prove to be prophetic during this year's

Year of the Ox. Make sure you take action to combat addictions. Speak up and say "No!" endless parties, alcohol smoking.

Chapter 3: Horoscope 2021 Aquarius By The Year Of Birth

Horoscope 2021 Aquarius - Ox
Aquarius-Ox 2021 won't face any issues with growth in the field of professional. He can create a successful career but to do this, the man will need to pushand work hard. In extending the circle of communications can play into your hands. Be open to meeting new people. It is also essential to understand how to plan your the time as well as energy. Experts advise planning the implementation of large-scale projects early in the spring. You should complete them by May and the result of your efforts will show in the autumn. You can spend your time working on your physical fitness. Regular exercise can also have an impact on your mental wellbeing.

Family Aquarius-Oxen need to be more attentive to their partner in order to build stronger romantic bonds. The free heart will meet destiny and leave behind oppressive solitude.

Horoscope 2021 Aquarius - Dragon

In 2021, Aquarius Dragon will be on the move a lot. Aquarius-Dragon will be a lively, conversations, and the chance to be close to powerful individuals. To others the person he is attractive. This, in conjunction with dedication and sociability is the key to being successful in the field of professional. A key aspect of this is the ability of the Aquarius Dragon to collaborate with people who are similar to them. Collaboration in 2021 is likely to yield better outcomes than individual efforts. This is especially true for those whose work is in the field of creativity.

People in search of an ideal partner will get over their loneliness. A fascinating person will be revealed in the vicinity of the Aquarius-Dragon who he would like to begin a family. If you've already fulfilled your destiny, be sure that your romantic relationship will grow stronger in 2021.

Horoscope 2021 Aquarius - Tiger

Aquarius Tiger in 2021 is suggested to increase their strength. Twelve months can be difficult. This is not the best moment to go on a holiday. It is time to put aside your mental peace. Do not be disappointed. The effort is worth the reward. It takes a lot of effort to get to success. Set yourself specific goals and set out to meet them. Show your manager that you are skilled and skilled enough to assume the responsibility for big tasks. Depend solely on your own abilities, your friends and colleagues won't be able assist you in any way.

In the personal realm it is a period of peace. The family Aquarius-Tiger will be in a position to breathe and unwind and relax. His companions will be there to embrace him with warm and loving care. If you're one of the lonely ones who are not looking for a partner, they ought to be looking at familiar acquaintances from the past. There is a chance that among them they'll discover an appropriate contender for being their spouse.

Horoscope 2021 Aquarius - Cat (Rabbit)
Aquarius Cat (Rabbit) will not have time to be bored after 2021. Each day will be exciting, bright filled with interesting and interesting events. Amazing ideas will sprout each day in the minds of the people who are part of this sign. You should try to put them

into practice. It will benefit both the entrepreneurs as well as those working for another. It is not advised to embark on something brand new just for those who aren't able to solve the problems of the past. Be sure to eliminate them before they take on massive proportions. Are you looking to change your job? Take your time and do not get unhappy if you weren't able to get the job you had hoped for. Don't let petty setbacks destroy your fuse.

In the daily life of Aquarius (Rabbit) dramatic changes are not to be expected that should not bring sadness to people who are empty.

Horoscope 2021 Aquarius - Snake

Aquarius snakes in 2021 need to stay on top of their game to ensure they don't be a victim of the opportunity to alter their lives. Don't be apprehensive that fate will be able to provide you with the life you've always wanted to. Prepare yourself to work to the max. Be a great employee on the professional level Don't regret the things that matter to you effort, time and effort. This is the time to not be lazy. This is a good time for activation. It Is necessary to be involved with the project in the beginning in the calendar year.

In your personal life, Aquarius Snake is advised to be active. Do not be afraid to accept the responsibility for people you love about. If you've been in a relationship for a long time it will help them move towards having a joyful family life. If you've already established your own family, you're now ready to fill it up. The announcement of the birth of your child could be a shocker however, you shouldn't be worried about this. Aquarius-Snake is preparing to become the parent of your dreams.

Horoscope 2021 Aquarius - Horse

The Aquarius-Horse of 2021 will need to put in the work. Get more engaged in the field of professional work. Change with the times or a change in speed of living. This is the key to positive changes. Don't be afraid of taking in new concepts. Whatever Aquarius Horse will do, Lady Luck will support him. You are welcome to show off your various abilities. Have you thought about making a go of it in the an entrepreneurial venture for an extended period of time? It's time to do it. To achieve success, you must establish specific goals for yourself and work towards them, and follow strictly to the program.

Personally, difficulties aren't anticipated. People who are close to family will feel the warmth and love of the other half. They will respond in friendly. Free Aquarius-Horse is likely to meet with a person is looking to have a child.

Horoscope 2021 Aquarius - Dog

The Aquarius-Dog won't be forced to lament the weakness in 2021. He will have the desire to do something, set ambitious goals for himself , and then achieve them while fully embracing his potential as a creative person. Achieving success is for those who do not hesitate, who are open to learning new things. This is an ideal time to self-study, as well as the execution of big-scale initiatives. Don't waste time or energy to accomplish this. Your efforts won't disappoint you. You will ultimately build your base of knowledge and secure yourself a professional progression.

In his private life, Aquarius-Dog is likely to take pleasure in the good fortunes of destiny. It will inspire those who are single seeking to begin an actual relationship, and begin an extended family soon. Families who will likely become parents by 2021, look forward to the positive feelings.

Horoscope 2021 Aquarius - Goat (Sheep)

Aquarius Goat (Sheep) from 2021 is expected to have the ability to improve their existing skills, learn additional ones as well as build many skills. In the workplace they will be indispensable in the first place as creators of new ideas. Don't be limited to planning, do your part, and try to carry out significant projects, regardless of how big and complicated they appear. This is how you can increase the base of your material. It is important to note that there is the possibility of a low probability that none of the Aquarius-Goats will be able to raise their wealth. If the lack of funds is a major issue you can seek help from family members.

When it comes to matters that concern the heart things will be effortless and tranquil. Family members must take a moment to concentrate on improving their home. For those who are free should be advised to not get too involved in flirting. Be sure to make a connection with the person who you truly enjoy.

Horoscope 2021 Aquarius - Rat

To the Aquarius Rats, 2021 is going to be bright and rich. There's no reason for you to be concerned. It's your moment, make the most of it. Use the energy available to create the most important channel. This is the right time to start working on those tasks that have previously seemed daunting to you. It is your right to tackle them even if they require the acquisition of new skills. A company to which you put your all into will eventually give you satisfaction but also a significant economic return. To accumulate capital, it will not be unnecessary to take business trips, and take on the responsibility in conducting important discussions.

In the life of the Aquarius-Rat they will be able to live without major issues. The Aquarius-Rat will be able to indulge in the romance of an intimate relationship with an ethereal partner. The idyll can last for many years when he doesn't talk often about it.

Horoscope 2021 Aquarius - Monkey

Experts believe that by 2021, Aquarius-Monkey should not be impeded from achieving their goals. To succeed, it's sufficient for them to be strong and consistent. Being able to protect your rights can be beneficial too. While doing this it is essential to remain honest. It is not advisable to create happiness by blaming another's loss Do not place an axle on the wheels of rivals and try to maintain positive relationships with them. In 2021, the Aquarians-Monkeys who are able to deal with emotions, manage their relationships and behave with prudence will be the best of Olympus. If you can plan smartly, you'll never be wrong.

In the personal world those who make time to do it will be fortunate and it will be hard to achieve. Don't overshadow the matters of your heart. Make the most of existing relationships or seek out new ones if you feel your heart is in peace.

Horoscope 2021 Aquarius - Rooster

The Aquarius-Rooster 2021 is nothing to be worried about. Luck is with him So, you should be bold, and take action in areas where you needed to back off. Don't give up, put in an excellent foundation for a successful future. People who work hard will be rewarded with a dazzling achievement.

When it comes to the profession, all will go in a positive way, but difficulties are not out of the question in the personal realm. They're waiting for the first time for those Aquarius-Roosters that are sluggish or predisposed. Don't go too high or you'll hurt yourself when you fall. Be kind and patient to your partner. Be wise. The lonely souls should take greater initiative. Make the first step toward an enjoyable future with someone who has been there for you.

Horoscope 2021 Aquarius - Pig (Boar)
The Aquarius-Pigs in 2021 (Boar) are likely to be successful. The future is bright for them, especially in the business world. In the first place, this is true for those who are a part with this sign, who're engaged doing their passions. It is easy for them to accomplish their goals. The results from their work will be beyond the expectations of everyone. Are you looking to switch jobs? Find the perfect job or to create your own business. No worries, whatever you choose you'll surely be with you. It is recommended to dedicate some time for professional growth and self-education.

In the realm of personal the Aquarius-Pig (Boar) can expect to experience peace and harmony. Men of the family will go on the second wedding anniversary, and will rekindle their passion for soulmate. If you're a single person the chance to meet for the first time is in store for their arrival. It's possible that by 2021, they'll walk across the aisle.

Chapter 4: Horoscope For January 2021
Aquarius

Aquarius In January of 2021, Aquarius will be searching for ways to achieve self-realization in a new way. The desire to know the unknown, to dive into mysticism , and to explore the realm of esotericism is just too big. It shouldn't be a surprise when during the Christmas season decorating the interior of your house with a symbol of symbol of talisman, a statue of bulls. Bull.

The January 2021 horoscope Aquarius promises many occasions, connections and outings. It's not like you need to be seated in one spot. With her charm There are people who share her interests. However, in the second part in the month your enthusiasm and energy will drop. Then you'll begin to get into your own thoughts and then escalate the situation. The practice of spirituality will be of huge benefits.

Aquarius can't imagine its existence without heroic efforts. Prepare yourself, as in January, there will be numerous unanticipated events you'll need to conquer by yourself. Get your courage together and take on the combat. The odds are in favor of those who do not scared of the trials of life. The most desirable traits are shown! Furthermore, Aquarius can become more determined and patient if she desires. In the end, don't create castles out of illusions. Be more real. Make sure you take an examination of your old and new acquaintances. There are some who are not willing to offer their help in tough times.

The January 2021 horoscope advises Aquarius to consider your finances and your career. You've been able to "grown" from being a basic employee. Now is the time to work towards the top place. However, be sure to behave in a manner that is calm and honest and don't go over your shoulders. There are some rules that shouldn't be violated, regardless of the reason.

Love Horoscope in January 2021 Aquarius
A lonely Aquarius is able to make with a nice person from the start of January 2021. You're so intelligent and friendly that no one is able to resist your charming smile. It's possible that romance will occur in a flash. The friendship will slowly develop into a

romantic relationship. Sharing interests, sympathy, and attraction is not something to run away from this. The feelings are evident and strong Be sincere.

However, you shouldn't ignore your loved ones and taking good care of them. Take time to be there for your family and friends. It is possible to establish a family company, and work closely with other experienced individuals. Make sure you are able to manage your emotions in a way you do not get lost in the pleasures of sensual love.

The love horoscope of Jan 2021 in Aquarius forecasts change in personal realm. It is recommended to avoid relationship that isn't trustworthy in order to avoid to be in a shambles. Even though, many won't be in romance, the process will take an enormous amount of effort and time. If you have to choose between a quiet and raucous communication and a tense relationship, you should choose the first. A relationship with a coworker or with someone who is already married cannot be prohibited. It is recommended to take care to conceal this from anyone else.

This January Aquarius is likely to think, reflect and enjoy a moment of relaxation in the natural world. The way you see the world will change and loneliness could result in unexpected discoveries. The world's beauty as well as the beauty of your own internal transformations will allow you understand yourself from a the brighter side. Spiritual growth is in the forefront. Don't forget to assist family members, be more compassionate and caring.

The month of January is 2021. Aquarius work and money

The January 2021 horoscope Aquarius recommends communicating "on business" and not chat with anyone. Collect information that will help you succeed in your job and professional growth. Make specific goals for achieving your goals. Think about the future in your mind. What does it offer you? If you're systematic and accountable, there is nothing that will disrupt the flow of your life. It is beneficial to create strategies that lead to opportunities.

The development of new ideas must push Aquarius to act. Changes in the world of work will only come about through the ability to think freely. Be mindful, don't get ahead of yourself, and keep track of what you come up with with creativity. The month of January is a good time to change jobs. If you're looking to be an entrepreneur take the time to gather the necessary paperwork.

Horoscope of January 20, 2021 suggests Aquarius to put money into profit-making projects. If this happens in the first week in the month the amount of money and interest will rise. However, you shouldn't rely on luck and fortune "from Heaven". You must work hard in order to make improvements to your financial position. Financial support from relatives and friends isn't an option.

In January, at the end, Aquarius can find a part-time job, or even a redemption. This will not affect the main task. A lot of people will get help from an individual who has the highest standing within society. However, keep this information hidden. Events and promotions that are charitable are also a great way to generate income and increase the budget, which can be surprising and enjoyable.

Health and movement during January 20, 2021. Aquarius

Horoscope for January 2021. Aquarius at the start of the month, predicts an unending flow of opportunities and energy. Particularly if you begin the path to health and strengthening your immune system. The right diet, exercising and a dose of positivity - this is the recipe for great overall health throughout the month.

Aquarius is likely to have to devote much of their time doing chores at home. If you're planning to remodel ahead, make sure you purchase everything you require for an event of a massive scale. In the end, don't think too far ahead, and tackle household problems quickly.

A lot of people can imagine that they are building a site, as the horoscope of January 2021 forecasts for Aquarius. Unfortunately, this isn't the most ideal month for construction, but you're brimming with confidence and power. Be aware of your mental state. family scandals and stress can happen. The possibility of trauma is not ruled out when you do not take care to be cautious. It is safer to avoid an extended drive in your vehicle.

New Moon to be in Capricorn 13 January 2021 for Aquarius

The January 2021 horoscope suggests Aquarius to take good proper care for their overall health. Massage, bath and hardening are extremely beneficial. Get rid of drinking and junk food Any vice can cause an addiction that is strong.

The New Moon, Aquarius will be able to generate more earnings however, only through honest methods. The need for profit and power will be high, and you'll need to take your time often. The money can "warm" your pockets however, do not rely on huge amounts. When you are in a difficult situation Do not be afraid to consult an experienced guide.

Aquarius is a sign that can cause a lot of issues in the family during January 20, 2021. The reason could be a variety of factors, including the loss of trust, long-running mistrust, and animosity. Don't try to flirt with your partner, as this could result in divorce.

Full Moon located in Leo on the 28th of January 2021 in Aquarius

The relationship between Aquarius and his spouse will be intense. The emotions and feelings can be difficult to manage. Be mindful not just of keeping your marriage intact but also your mental well-being. Regularly sexy conversations and scandals that are conducted with a high volume will negatively impact your immune system.

The January 2021 horoscope recommends Aquarius to select strategies that will lead to peaceful relationship in the presence of loved ones. Make an effort to be flexible to the things that can't be altered in your relationship. It is important to be patient to use when communicating.

On the day of a Full Moon, Aquarius cannot claim to be healthy. As chronic diseases come back to their own, and you'll have visit the doctor. If you stick to the prescribed regimen, get more rest and do not let yourself down due to minor issues and everything will work out.

Most favorable dates of in January for Aquarius 5-7 14, 24, 29,

The Horoscope of February 20, 2021 Aquarius

The forecast for the horoscope of February 2021 for Aquarius warns that the cause for many of the issues he'll face is his own insanity. Don't focus on the inner voice of yours telling you. There are times when he isn't always right. It's his fault. may trust unfriendly people and be fooled. You can also make the first impression of other people.

Prepare yourself for the change. Start by implementing them yourself. Begin with an image, then you can move to the manner of communicating with half, friends, family members, and colleagues.

Concentrate on ways to alter your life in this manner. Don't be rushed into changing your life completely, in order that in the end , you will not regret it in the future. Take your time, and rely on your intuition.

By February 20, Aquarius begins to listen to his inner voice. Aquarius is reminded about the need to boost self-esteem, and to improve his own self-esteem for the purpose of building self-confidence.

The stars are aligned on the side of the people who represent this sign. With their assistance they will be more assertive and others will admire their strength.

The Horoscope for February 2021- Aquarius indicates that they'll eventually want to be leaders. This is a good thing in the field of work.

You are free to showcase your strengths. Be confident by doing this. Show that you're worthy of the position, and take responsibility for the execution of crucial initiatives.

Your own personal interests should be the first priority when you are working. Act decisively.

Don't worry, your colleagues won't be affected. Like you, they will be focussed on their own professional development. Aquarius is able to overtake them if he is able to draw interest from his employer.

In your personal life, grave problems aren't expected. Your friends will view you to be a kind and generous person. This characteristic will become more evident and you'll be able to forgive your errors and mistakes.

It's great, but you should not take it too far. Aquarius February 2021, isn't the right opportunity to make use of your power as well as authority and confidence of other people. You can't do anything just to earn the spotlight and fame.

Love Horoscope in February 2021 Aquarius

Take advantage of the luck of the draw as the chance to deal with the most difficult issues in your personal life. Put your mind into a fist and mark the "i" with the letter s. It will need to be accomplished, even for Aquarius who's romantic relationship was secret, and the ones who had to end it with the breakup. If your love for one is present and strong, then reconnect with your loved one. Don't hide your shame that your relationship is coming in the end. Do not lie to your ex and she will offer you the chance to start with a fresh start.

Consider her kindness as an act of kindness from above. Thank her and make sure not to repeat the mistakes you made later on. Be more active, less talk. Let your partner know that you're willing to transform for the benefit of a happy and prosperous future together. Horoscope for February 2021. Aquarius is not a good time to be relying on a speedy outcome. It is possible to restore confidence of the half in time, but be patient.

Individuals who have this sign will be more attractive to the eyes of other people. This is not a accidental. They are actively involved in a transformation of their image. They want to appear perfect. This is relevant for women and males. They shouldn't be ashamed of it.

A desire for pleasing other people is common. Aquarius males do not have to be concerned about their appearance. They may also put the bet on bravery patience, kindness, and respect when it is appropriate. Women can make use of weapons like fashionable items including accessories, makeup and accessories accentuating their beauty.

If you are an Aquarius who are looking to improve their life the love horoscope of February 2021 suggests being aware of your mood. The Aquarius must be positive.

Believe that the changes you want to see positive for you are on the horizon and will surely arrive at you.

January 2021 Aquarius work Money, work

Creative professionals must take advantage of the time when luck is on their side, and display to others in their vicinity their abilities as well as the results of perseverance.

The business community, especially those who are directly linked to the field of art are also expected to become more involved.

In the workplace, Aquarius will also benefit by the perception of other people, they are attractive. People will be attracted by them. There will be many who are able to point out new income sources.

Choose those that permit you to apply your expertise and knowledge. However be aware that you shouldn't assume that everything will be served before you in a silver plate. The horoscope for February 2021. Aquarius suggests making every effort to expand your area of influence.

To build the foundation of your material keep yourself a fervent lover of everything.

When you can, start collecting expensive items. Make investments in the preservation of treasured heirlooms.

If this isn't appealing to you, you can use the your free money to establish an additional branch, or expand the scope of your business. Aquarius who aren't associated with the entrepreneurial venture should invest in improving their living circumstances.

Health and movement during February 2021 Aquarius

The beginning of this month expected to be difficult. Accidents or illnesses that Aquarius's family members will suffer could cause stress. Help them by helping Aquarius's relatives. Encourage them to put off until later the activities that threaten their safety or well-being.

Careful and cautiousness will not harm yourself. Take care to prevent serious injuries. Reduce conflicts to shield yourself from the harmful results of stress. This is particularly true for children who experience the pressure of parents and grandparents.

Horoscope for February 2021. Aquarius will be a delight to you with the information that his body will be robust enough to handle the exacerbation of chronic ailments.

The energy will be so high that it's not an immoral act to take advantage of this. Put your energy into the realization of those plans you had previously put off due to various reasons. It's possible that a portion of the time will have to be put into the renovation of your home as well as other chores for the household.

Impact of the New Moon in Aquarius February 11, 2021, on Aquarius

The first thing this New Moon will affect in the life of an Aquarius is his appearance. It will be brighter and attractive to other people. This can be utilized not only in private life however, but also in the workplace.

But, don't be relying solely on your own charisma. Accept what you value most fully, and learn how to keep yourself motivated, stay determined. With this, you'll be able to achieve your goals.

Horoscope for February 2021. Aquarius will also suggest focusing on their prudence and capability to control not only them, but also the people who are around them. This will help his favour in the financial industry. Capital growth is affected in part by the securing of professions in the field.

Enjoy your time off not just with your family as well as with yourself, and your well-being, and even your psychological. It's an excellent idea to take an excursion.

The impact of the Full Moon in Virgo on February 27, 2021, on Aquarius

The full moon can allow Aquarius along with other zodiac signs to look at things they typically do not notice. Maybe some of them will be able to see that they aren't sacrificed enough to them.

Instead of dwelling about it and thinking negative thoughts You need to look at your behavior. Look at ways you can improve your relationships with family and friends.

The February 2021 horoscope advises Aquarius to take advantage of the perfect time for transformation. But, other aspects such as the financial sphere must not be ignored as well. It is suggested to switch into the economic mode to ensure that in case of unexpected costs you won't be found in the middle.

It is best to take time to improve your living conditions. It is not required to start repairs. A simple rearrangement should suffice.

The most favorable days in February 2021 Aquarius The Aquarius day is: 1, 4 5, 15, 26,

Chapter 5: Horoscope For The Month Of March 2021 Aquarius

The March 2021 horoscope Aquarius promises a ambiguous time. On one hand, you'll become more sensible, serious contemplating the future However, on the flip side you won't be able to resist your desire to appear wealthy. To make an impression on the people in his vicinity, Aquarius is likely to begin buying expensive clothing and luxury goods, all in order to concentrate on his appearance.

The money in March 2021 is likely to disappear quickly. Begin saving now if you don't wish to be uncomfortable in the financial world. Learn to manage your finances prudently. The future of stability in the material world is for those who take care to think over every decision they make.

In his spare time it is recommended for Aquarius to reflect on the events that occurred in the last weeks. Make the right decisions or rationalize your feelings, and attempt to unleash your imagination.

Rely on your intuition But take into consideration your peers' opinions in order to prevent provoking conflict. Don't pressure your loved ones by imposing authority. Prepare to cooperate. Individual work in the spring is not likely to bring desired results for Aquarius.

Aquarius February 2021 Love Horoscope

In March's early and mid-March the need to convey your feelings and feelings however you can get more intense. This Aquarius February 2021 love horoscope suggests that the person who is a victim of love will need to spend money. A large amount will be spent on gifts for your loved people. To surprise those whom you love dearly it's not an issue. Furthermore, you'll get nothing less than a pleasant experience as a reward. Most of the time Aquarius is not known to utilize his wealth to improve his relationships with other people, however when spring arrives it will be a time to change. Cash for Aquarius from March 2021 is likely to prove to be a great instrument to strengthen relationships and there's nothing wrong in it. In the time of the transit of Venus it is nothing to discuss about something sacred and wonderful.

According to the horoscope of the month of March in 2021 Aquarius at the close of March will bring to the forefront of relationships with family, colleagues and friends. They will also be a source of support for neighbors. Make them more trusting and friendly. It isn't recommended to concentrate on this topic solely for lonely hearts looking for the possibility of a second chance. Aquarius in March is bound to meet his end if he does not remain at home. Make a habit of it, and be open to making new friends. A trip of a short duration or a shorter vacation abroad is an excellent idea. April 2021, Aquarius Work and money

In the initial half of March the horoscope for March 2021 suggests Aquarius to be reliant on their creativity and entrepreneurship and the capacity to stay mentally active for a prolonged duration. However you should not physically rest. Aquarius is required to be in good physical condition so that you can be able to host all planned business meetings. Be proactive and start the conversation with the people who can assist you in solving your issues.

It's the time to establish new important contacts. It's possible to bring those who are right for you into your life when you show to them your intelligence and the capability to stand up to intense competition in the realm of intellectuals.

Build relationships with people who can help you create a an enduring foundation for the future you want to live in. But, don't believe that you will get the things you desire only with the assistance of other people. Aquarius will try to make every situation to their advantage. To do this, it's sufficient to be pragmatic and rational. There is no problem when due to the passage of Mercury. With the influence on this planet as per the Horoscope for March 2021 Aquarius It will be simple to improve current professional skills and learn new information like sponges.

This will have a positive effect on the overall condition of the base material. There is a chance to boost the cost column, and purchase new equipment, and other things that can't be replaced in everyday life. There will be funds to update your wardrobe, and for purchasing fresh food items that will nourish your mind and and in particular for books.

Are you worried that these costs could affect your financial security? Find alternative sources of income. The experts suggest that Aquarius begin teaching and explore the possibility of becoming a writer or lecturer.

The March 2021 horoscope suggests Aquarius to focus on the remaining of the month working on finances. In order to resolve any problems that arise be practical Try to implement fresh, exciting ideas, old ideas well-thought out strategies.

If you need to make sure you are in a good place, and start searching for a part-time work or a new sources of revenue. If you require assistance, require it, talk to your neighbors, friends, relatives.

It's not going to be feasible to accumulate a substantial amount of money at the beginning of spring. The March 2021 horoscope of Aquarius is preparing for the fact that he'll need to pay off all of his savings in one go. The astrologers will be leaving to improve their health, or to travel urgently. A portion of the money are to be used for the legal backing of transactions that are important.

Health and movement in March 2021 Aquarius

Horoscope for March 2021. Aquarius is delighted by the knowledge that this month he'll have the chance to focus on the activities that give satisfaction. A lot of people will join dancing, participate in sporting events, and then begin regular exercises at home. There's enough energy to take part in competitions where Aquarius will likely to produce positive results.

In March, in addition to other things, the need for expression will increase. If you follow the prompts of your soul and it's likely to take you to Aquarius to a workshop in art with a drama group, and so on. Don't be afraid to do something you've never attempted before. When you are in the realm of art you can achieve the same results like in sports. Explore your creative side and see the positive impact it has on your attitude.

The March 2021 horoscope for Aquarius suggests that the start of spring will turn you into true adventurers. As the seasons change women will notice how their attraction to sexuality of the opposite intensifies. They'll be more active. It's possible that at the end, many decide to have a baby.

Impact on The New Moon in Pisces March 13 2021 Aquarius

The horoscope for the month of March 2021 will prepare Aquarius for the time where he will reassess all that was once important to Aquarius. It is also worth making use of to alter your perspective on money, to master the art of managing it effectively. Develop yourself to accumulate capital, decrease the risk of losing huge sums.

For the next two weeks, in the professional world, Aquarius will have to work closely with colleagues. They will share the responsibility of conducting business negotiations, the development of large-scale plans as well as plans for investments. The March 2021 teamwork period could be your opportunity to move further up the ladder of success build your foundation of materials.

In this New Moon period in March it is expected that work will come out at the top of the list for Aquarius However, the personal aspects is not to be neglected. Find a way to strike a harmony between personal and professional obligations. You must work hard to achieve the job that you are drawn to but do not ignore the other half that is who needs affection and love.

The influence of Full Moon in Libra on March 28, 2021 in Aquarius

The full moon is the reason for this. the Horoscope for March 2021 suggests that Aquarius be patient for any changes to education, particularly in the field of professional particularly regarding international partnership, legal issues.

Be aware of the chances you have to build the foundations for a successful future. This time, Aquarius will be focused on his profession that is true but you should not let your life dictate your destiny. It is a time when crucial decisions need to be made.

The month of March in 2021 will be the time when lots of will need to fight for a romantic connection or end the relationship if there's no chance of forming a relationship. Before deciding to burn bridges take a look at the advantages and disadvantages, think about the scenarios that could arise.

Aquarius is advised to spend time with family members, particularly with his brothers and sisters who is a lot of fun.

Most favorable days that will be in the month of March 2021 to Aquarius 2-7 12 18, 26

Chapter 6: Horoscope For April 2021
Aquarius

The horoscope of April 2021 to Aquarius warns that Aquarius has a chance to broaden his scope of influence. To do this, you'll have to step out of that comfort zone and show your various talents, and start making your voice heard regardless of whether it is against the general consensus.

External conditions can play your hand The concepts of Aquarius will be welcomed with open arms and all issues that are controversial are able to be debated, forming an open and constructive dialog. It's time to push for greater, to advance. Luck will be with those who are observant and shrewd, making the most of the opportunities that the universe provides him.

The fact that during mid-month Aquarius is able to reach new heights in his professional and social realm is not a sign that Aquarius will not have time to relax and enjoy. This time it is likely that you will be able to find a compromise between what you require and what you wish to accomplish.

April is also known as positive because of the location of the celestial body. Thanks to this, Aquarius becomes an independent, courageous hard-working, genuine enthusiast.

The horoscope for April 2021 states, Aquarius will open up new perspectives in nature of leadership. This will enable him to excel within his industry, develop new abilities, and gain the latest knowledge which is crucial for growth.

For personal matters In this case, the focus should be placed on connections to blood relations, even distant ones. Spend time giving them a helping hand, and to show them with your affection. It's not necessary to take a trip with your loved ones, when you go on a trip even only for a brief period of time.

Aquarius April 2021 Love Horoscope
In the course of the transition from Venus into the signification in Aries, Aquarius will feel his relationships grow more vibrant and intense. Through this period the Aquarius

will be more spontaneous and flexible, and ready to show his emotions in many ways.

Your partner will be able to enjoy pleasant surprise every day It is a fact that you are sure to love this kind of situation. This will help your relationship to become stronger. But, it must be acknowledged that the passage of Venus is not going to be beneficial to all.

The April 2021 horoscope of Aquarius warns that certain members that belong to the sign particularly the ones who are colder emotionally are likely to withdraw and are liable to be the victims of unfounded anxiety. One of these is the worry that your spouse isn't considering you as a serious person.

Due to this, Aquarius could begin to appear unproductive, believing that Aquarius does not place any burdens on the other half, and maintains the sense of self-worth. But the person you love will see the situation in a different way in view of the partner's behaviour as indicates an absence of affection. For certain couples, this can refer to only one thing: the distance between them and their break.

Are you still lonely? The love horoscope of April 20, 2021, will remind Aquarius that he won't be fated to stay at home. Engage with people more often, take part in showing your love Don't be afraid to express your feelings and don't be scared of rejection.

If you began relationships relatively recently you should learn how to have an open dialog with your partner. Discuss your experiences with them, otherwise you'll be with a sense of complete solitude.

The 14th of April is a good day to strengthen relationships with your offspring, grandparents as well as other family members. The April 2021 horoscope recommends Aquarius to focus more on loved onesbecause, when the time comes to face hardship they'll be the first to be prepared to assist you.

Aquarius was always a focus on family and values for the family and family values, so it is not surprising that the aspect must be given prioritised in the second quarter of April is not a concern for Aquarius. But, it won't be easy to switch completely to daily living, home and communications with family members. You'll be juggling this with your work obligations. Try to keep your perfect balance.

April 2021 Aquarius Work money

The first part in the month could cause Aquarius to be decisive and swift in their actions. Haste is not a necessity in the case of expanding the business sphere of influence, but it is recommended to decline it by writing or signing crucial documents.

The April 2021 Horoscope advises Aquarius working with paper take time to carefully look over all the small details. Look over the words written in small font, then analyze the writing. Don't let detractors fool you.

If you are looking for luck that is unpredictable it is in the favor of Aquarians who's profession is connected to sales. Businessmen also have luck. They'll have the chance to make deals that are profitable and contracts that will result in huge profits for Aquarius in the near future.

He'll be able achieve new heights due to his eloquence and also the capacity to transition from words to actions within a short period of time. If you are looking for the ideal job, they'll not be with no luck. April is the best month to attend interviews. In the realm of finance it is unlikely to be a issue as long as you're vigilant with your investments. If you encounter sudden financial difficulties, don't get worried. The April 2021 horoscope is a reminder to Aquarius that he is able to depend on his family members.

Beginning on April 19th, you'll be spending longer inside those walls that surround your personal home. This isn't an excuse to abandon your business activities. Aquarius can be involved in important projects at a distance. The same way it is feasible to conclude agreements, negotiate or agreements.

What you need to be the most attentive to is the issue of money. In the interim cut down on purchases you have not planned particularly large ones. In the meantime, switch to economy mode, beware of temptations, to which could cost you an enormous amount. Do you want to increase your capital? Do your best to implement business concepts that originate in your mind.

Health and movement in April 2021. Aquarius

The social world will be first. To be successful you must do your best every day, travel for business Pay attention to the smallest the smallest of details. There is no time to rest or in other words.

Aquarius is active physically as well as intellectually. There are times when he feels exhausted, but that doesn't mean that he does not provide him with pleasure. But, to carry on doing what you love you must properly disperse forces. Additionally during between spring and summer you should be aware of any injuries, and stay focused in the rear of the vehicle.

Aries New Moon April 12, 2021 for Aquarius

The April 2021 horoscope of Aquarius warns us that during this New Moon period he will come up with interesting and unique ideas in a series. This is not the right moment to put off the implementation of these ideas until later. In the present you have the chance to enhance your standing on the social scene.

This is possible through the reconnection with powerful personalities. Open yourself to meeting new people, enticed deals, accepting which Aquarius will easily transform their lives for the better.

Your fate will delight you with the prospect of new possibilities. Take advantage of them without fretting the possibility that your choice may be difficult to comprehend for those who are close to you. It's always been difficult for people to accept Aquarius as they are, but that isn't an excuse to alter and adjust to the other.

Yet it is important to move forward no matter the views of others isn't an excuse to destroy bridges. Make sure you maintain a positive relation with all those you value. Accept criticism with a calm attitude.

Full Moon located in Scorpio on April 27, 2021, for Aquarius

Full moons are the perfect time to take a leap of faith. But, only those who can ask the right questions can be competent to do it. Feeling dissatisfied? Look into the root of your problem.

Maybe the main issue is that you're high-stressed on yourself. It's time to make a change and to take action.

With the help by the moon's fullness, Aquarius can experience a greater determination to go on a journey, achieve new heights in the professional realm, and fulfill their goals. The pursuit of money, work, and pleasure in life will be brought into focus however, this does not mean you'll be able to forget about what you do for a living. It is good to know that no issues are anticipated in this field. This can be utilized to strengthen the romantic connection.

The most favorable days that will be in the month of April 2021 to Aquarius 1st, 7th 14, 18, 22,

Chapter 7: The Fixed Sign Characteristics Of The Aquarians

If you look at the Horoscope at the 12 houses, each one falls into either one of two categories: a moveable sign, fixed sign or dual sign. The chart below clearly clarifies what is moveable as well as fixed, and which are dual.

* Aquarius falling under the fixed signification, it makes Aquarians to be steady and determined about their choices.

They are grounded and practical in their dealings.

"Steadiness." is their guiding principle to achieve any goal in life.

* They are rational and logical thinkers which allows them to consider the future in advance to plan to ensure a better future.

The rigid nature makes them extremely rigid and unalterable and resists any change in the shortest time possible.

They are honest, trustworthy and loyal. This is a very reliable sign that allows them a lot of good acquaintances.

An example of a Perfectionist is Aquarians"; this is the word we should apply to them as

they're always searching for truth until the very end.
* They are excellent models of idealists too.

The Airy sign of Aquarians
A horoscope can be divided into four components of the natural world. Each sign has the characteristics of air, earth, and water. Aquarius is a sign of airy aspect of the sign. Therefore, we'll look at the airy characteristics of Aquarians.
* Airy signs are upward-moving in nature. Therefore, the Aquarians are extremely clever in nature. Their minds are extremely sharp, and the majority of geniuses belong to this category.
This is an indication that they are not connected to emotional attachments. They do possess emotions, but are detached in their behavior.
They are sensitive and objective when it comes to taking decisions.
* They are at a separation from emotionally dependent individuals. They are independent and appreciate the feeling of being completely alone

As previously mentioned, they're not emotionally oriented and aren't as passionate.

Because they are airy, they are extremely far-sighted and observant.

* Due to this sign's airy appearance, they appear very immature, cold, and eccentric

* They've got a attractive personality, but when they become upset and angry it can be very difficult to persuade them.

The traits of the SATURN are present in the Aquarians

The planet that governs Aquarius. Aquarius Sign can be described as The SATURN. Therefore, Saturn's hard performing qualities for a large cause are evident in these people.

The purpose of Lord Saturn is to create awareness of the karma and to enjoy the taste of the fruits of their work. Saturn is a planet of hard-core that represents the idea that whatever you offer, you need to receive it back.

Aquarians aren't a fan of having being in crowds. they prefer to work in their own way and are able to work for a an important cause.

* They are very difficult and difficult to comprehend due to the strong dominance qualities of Saturn that are similar to duty-mindedness, loneliness rigid and disciplined, and will bring about a permanent outcome.

They aren't able to express their affections or sympathy in public They look stylish and keep their emotions secret. Therefore, many people are misguided by their behavior and believe they're self-centered and arrogant.

* As a result of the attributes of Saturn they are viewed as dogmatic, unorthodox as well as outdated in their method of thinking.

They are selfless and apathetic when working making them famous. They leave a lot for the world prior to their death.

* The revolutionary and rebellious qualities of Saturn cause them to fight and support causes that are humanitarian without relying on profits.

Another important aspect that we should discuss is the field of work that they can do well. They are ideal for those fields that require persistence.

The ones that can achieve impossible feats through their constant dedication and dedication to completing the project.

The Aquarian Traits

So far, we've been able to understand the various aspects of Aquarius through the analysis of the individual elements. The next step is to look at the Aquarius as a whole , mixing all these elements into one. It's like giving combinations that give that unique characteristic of their character.

Unpredictable

As they are airy and fixed, their mental capacities are developed and pushed to think to the very extreme.

Their actions are therefore unpredictably for normal people.

Social

They employ a well-balanced method of keeping contact with friends. They are the people anyone can contact for assistance in the event of an emergency.

Intelligent

They are among the most educated people, with a sharp and imaginative brain that can analyze information quickly. They have the ability to be classified under the categories of genius and intellectuals.

Risk takers

Aquarians are risk-averse because they are very experimental with all things to uncover the secrets of life without worry, in a place that is impossible for ordinary people to achieve. This is what led them to discover a variety of things in the world.

Philosophical

Philosophers of all kinds are in this category, as their perspective on life from a distance brings them in close contact with their personal self. In addition, their continual pursuit to addressing the problems of other people to create an improved world allows them to comprehend the self more deeply, which is what makes them philosophical.

Diplomatic

Their calm and friendly nature made them excel as diplomats. Their skills in communication and the ability to think from different angles helped them become good Diplomats.

Communicative

They're very open to express their thoughts in their words, which truly enthrall many. They are skilled speakers and orators.

Revolutionary

They are extremely rebellious and at-risk when it comes to finishing projects that has deadlines. This makes them appear as revolutionary.

Farsightedness

They possess a unique ability to sense which allow them to anticipate what will happen ahead of time what will happen. Their ability to think ahead about the future has made them extremely shrewd individuals.

Sturdy

In terms of stubbornness, they are among the hardest people to convince. Aquarians are extremely argumentative by their behavior. It's very difficult to convince them they constantly prove they're correct.

Insensitive

If they encounter problems, they fix the issue. They don't look to lean on someone else's shoulder. They will simply distance themselves from their surroundings to seek the solution. They're airy which means they are less passionate and emotional.

However, that doesn't mean they aren't emotional. They are people who have less emotion and who are very practical, critical and odd. They tend to be more conceptual than pragmatic.

Broad-minded

They're very open-minded and will not perform actions solely to impress others or enhance their image. Their sharp mind is constantly searching for new opportunities to help fill in the gaps of the abyss.

Independent

They cherish freedom and freedom. They are also willing to give that same to their fellow citizens in transactions. Their kindness and generosity allow them be open to new ideas.

Bossy

They're the most difficult bosses you've encountered on the planet. Their decisions are incomprehensible to their subordinates. It's impossible to know if you will be promoted or dismissed in the event that you work under them. The only way to be successful to remain respectful and humble when you require a favor.

The strongest

Aquarians are the most self-confident people because they are self-confident, fun, and disconnected. They're at their most effective when they are left alone.

Aquarius Father characteristics

If the father of your child is Aquarian you can count on him to be supporter in all challenges.

He's always a great listener to his kids and might look cool out even if they make statements that could cause some horror for others.

He is patient when it comes to raising his children and pushing their child's talents to the next level. He offers a lot of liberty for his children to pursue their dreams without forcing their own ideas or goals.

Aquarian fathers are amazing in the sense that they are the main source of their children's support to help them face the world with confidence whenever the need arises.

What else could a child expect from the father of his child if he turns out to be the most trusted mentor and philosopher by providing a touch of help.

Children will be impressed by his ideas and his creativity as his genius attracts the attention of children, and there is it is no doubt that he is the hero and the ideal option to help children in their journey.

Aquarius Mother characteristics

The most gorgeous gift from God to Aquarian mothers will be their child. Children are what they are in their entire world. Whatever you can offer to them that is as precious as diamonds, their children are the first and most important top priority.

They are able to go in any way to meet their children's wants and wishes. They do not pamper their children, instead , they offer plenty of choice and freedom to choosing their own outfit to their hair style.

As mothers, they work to get them to stand on their own feet. They are taught things that they did not know prior to for the sake of helping children with their academics.

Although strict in regards in to disciplining their children, will clearly explain the reason and consequences of convincing their children that they are within the right place.

Aquarius Husband characteristics

He is a faithful husband, friend, and lover of his wife. He does not attempt or try to dominate his wife and he will not allow his wife to control himbecause being an independent man, is what gives his wife substantial freedom to make decisions but yet is a fan of his own autonomy and freedom, which is why we could describe him as an acquaintance than a romantic.

He is sincere and honest when it comes to his wife. Like I said, it is an obvious sign that he is an intelligent man and also loves an intelligent spouse. In order to impress him, his wife has to be smart in dealing with the world, and not having to deal with him.

He is understanding and compassionate and therefore never tries to force his wife to do anything she does not want in doing and also does not force his opinion on her in order to get tasks done.

One can imagine what an airy sign would be, one that is less emotional and cool when it comes to dealings. Therefore, do not expect an Aquarian husband to get henpecked. He is not a fan of being dependent. The only way to attract his attention is to show your sharp mind, which could outdo his standard of intelligence that he doesn't reveal.

He is equally devoted to his wife and provides a variety of surprise gifts with gifts for her. Be prepared for that when the husband you love is Aquarian.

Aquarius Wife traits

She is a loyal spouse to her husband, but she is also very independent and does not rely on her husband for the performance of her obligations.

As a detached woman, she lives her own life, not relying too much on her husband's income.

She is willing to help alleviate the burden and suffering of the family, without making a complaint or seeking assistance.

She is extremely nice to all who come across within the family. She has few friends in the outside world, but she is at being friendly to husband's friends.

She is a loving mother to her children However, she's not too emotionally for them. She offers plenty of love and assistance to her husband.

She is a passionate lover and a great companion to her husband. She does not impose his will on him but gives him the freedom to create his own choices.

The unique characteristic of an Aquarian wife is her multi-tasking capability and quick adaptation to any situation easily.

She is a smart spouse to her husband, who is able to manage her family well even even in the most difficult situations.

Aquarius Male characteristics

An Aquarian male always shows unpredictable behavior. In fact, the character of this sign is hidden.

They are introverts and extremely calm in their outlook. Due to the non-emotional nature of this sign, they are able to appear calm and serene in the midst of their daily life's turbulences.

They can handle life with ease, as they are sincere and honest when they approach things from a distance that allows them find the right solution to any issue.

Although they cherish their loved ones deeply in their hearts, they don't reveal it or show their feelings in a film manner. This is among the main characteristics of Aquarians which should be taken note of.

He is always content to be alone during times of crisis as they can disconnect themselves from their surroundings to examine the situation in the present and try to resolve the issue.

One of the most important things that Aquarian people, particularly males demonstrate is that they are specific in selecting their friends. They don't allow friends that disrupt or disturb them. They have the capacity of being able to observe others' actions without judging them.

Aquarius female traits

A Aquarian female is gorgeous with slightly medium to tall height, often with a moderately likable personality with fair skin. They have a stunning their appearance and are identifiable quickly in crowds.

The woman of Aquarius is extremely Intelligent and extremely secretive. Even the most intimate of friends of her can't know her next moves.

Typically, they shift the family responsibility on their shoulders much earlier in their lives and sometimes delay their marriage by a considerable amount of time to allow them to meet the family obligations first before they begin their lives in the future.

They prefer a man who is intelligent for their spouse with attractive appearance. Sometimes, they get married to someone who is not part of their caste or community, which causes a lot of trouble in the family, but she won't allow her to change her mind. Because they are obstinate and difficult to make changes to their decision they have made their final decision and feel they are more knowledgeable than other person in deciding what they want to do.

A woman who is Aquarian is extremely self-sufficient and practical. They enjoy freedom even after marriage, as they think marriage is necessary that is necessary for a society to live in peace However, inside they are disengaged and love their private life. In essence, they aren't much more emotional in relationships , when compared with other sign-women.

The style of their clothes is distinct and unique. They are fashionable in western clothing, and yet, they adhere to the traditional way of life.

Aquarius Child-like traits

Parents are always at ease with their child especially if they were born with the Aquarius sign. Because they are smart honest, sincere, and straight-forward in their character who offer lots of assistance during times of need.

They have an extremely wide-ranging perspective and are the most suitable member of the family to talk about issues in a relaxed manner with them.

A Aquarian child is never looking for help, in fact, they solve their issues at their own level. They are clever and savvy in recognizing the needs of others.

Being born with Intelligence is a natural ability, so it is a must to you will excel in your studies, unless there are powerful negative planetary influences that are associated with the 4th house on their chart.

They have a quick grasp of the things they see around them and can therefore anticipate or anticipate what might happen in a way that can be awe-inspiring to those who are around them.

The analysis they make on any topic of study due to their intense involvement, which is a key Saturn's characteristic that can make them excellent at studying with little effort.

Aquarius Lover traits

In line with their characteristic trait of putting everything into their work and giving 100% in any activity they engage in. They're quiet but romantic They are extremely compassionate and give their all to make their loved ones satisfied.

Because of their emotional disconnect, they can be at peace in their own space, even when their partner is in the same space and this can lead to an impression of not really caring to the other partner.

Their affection for their partner is sincere, however, they appear nice in their appearance. Only through careful observation will be able to discern their affection. However, if they are in love, they're the ideal to make their spouses happy and delight them in a variety of ways.

If you inquire about what they're looking for in a person it's not necessarily the physical appearance on the outside nor the way you dressed your home or how you think. They are more interested in the truth of you through their brains.

The Aquarius love affair begins with those who are smart and have amazing IQ abilities. Then is the physical appearance. Attraction can only happen when you can communicate with them on the level of intellect, not just through physical appearance.

They appreciate the modesty when they are approached to ask for help. People born under this sign tend to be extremely honest and sincere , and will offer all their dedication and devotion to their loved ones.

Aquarius Employee characteristics

Aquarians are ideal for jobs that require intelligence and brains However, they aren't suited for work that involves physical exercise. Therefore, for this reason they look lazy inwards however their brains are operating at the speed of light, which can lead to exhaust them quickly.

They are extremely hardworking and will leave no work to go unfinished. They're the greatest when they are finding the answers to the problems that arise in their work. They can achieve greater heights within an extremely short amount of time. Jobs that are creative usually suit for them because their mind is extremely creative and has many ideas and likes to explore new ideas every single day.

They can be great leaders, who can aid their coworkers. However, they can be difficult to understandbecause they perceive certain things in their own ways that cannot be recognized by people who are not who are around them.

The rest of the world is unable to form a firm opinion about Aquarian's mood since they are way ahead of the curve in their thinking and appear cool, which is impossible to detect their minds' work.

They're social however, they're isolated. They avoid bored people. They appear strange in their thinking, however they're organized.

Aquarius compatibility attributes

If it comes to compatibility, they're most in compatibility with Aries, Gemini, Libra and Sagittarius people born in the sign of Sagittarius.

They may feel difficult to work with Taurus and Cancer, Virgo and Pisces.

Other signs like Leo, Scorpio, Capricorn are somewhat compatible.

Aries and Aquarius

The most common elements between them is independence and having freedom.

They both love adventure and having amusement. They are a great pair since they share the same intellect.

They can be found at the mental level of comprehension and easily turn into an ideal acquaintance.

Aries is an ebullient sign, which is also a fiery sign. Aquarius has a soaring sign. So, guess what happens when you add air to the flame! It is extremely windy and can reach the heights. This is exactly what happens when it comes to this type of relationship If they respects each other.

On the negative side, the disconnection of Aquarius emotionally may create a lot of pain for Aries. However, the Aries must recognize it's the Aquarius characteristic to be disengaged.

Gemini and Aquarius

It's another fascinating pair who enjoys being in one another's company. The two are a perfect match since they both love to try the new and are awed by the thrill of adventure. They do not like following the rules or rules to live their life to the fullest. Therefore, what could hinder them in the event that they meet!

They are attracted to each other very often.

Both of them can leap up at a high level of intellectual comprehending any topic.

Libra and Aquarius

A pair that hangs on for a long period of time. Libra loves the sharp-witted Aquarius and Aquarius also is drawn to Libra's charismatic actions at the intellectual levels.

They both enjoy travel and communicating with people and are interested in their artistic talents and other activities that expand their knowledge.

They can collaborate well to complete any human wellbeing project and accomplish their objectives.

It's a great combination helping to lift the community for a cause.

Sagittarius and Aquarius

Another great Aquarius partner to enjoy chats and conversations is Sagittarius. They are both less emotional and they are able to appreciate each other's practical way of doing things. Aquarius prefers Sagittarius thinking broadly and Sagittarius appreciate Aquarius the individuality and freedom of living life to the fullest.

Chapter 8: Aquarius Personality

Personality Profile

The Aquarius focus on human values which makes them excellent partners in relationships. However, there's one drawback. Aquarians aren't able to love someone because they are unable to convey their emotions. They are naturally reserved and do not like to show the emotions they feel on their sleeve. Since they keep their personal lives concealed, Aquarius can appear eccentric to those who don't know their personalities. However Aquarius is a person who Aquarian is a person who thinks and lives at many levels, particularly at multiple levels of the mind.

The Aquarius are an intriguing mix of intellect and quirky. They're friendly and have an unwavering love for humanity in general and are able to commit their lives to a specific type of mission that will helping humanity. Aquarians are great for these kinds of jobs and functions due to various reasons. they thrive in teams They are awed by thinking of large ideas, they search at real-world solutions and develop solutions that are innovative and effective They reject intolerance and discrimination, they possess an unrivaled ability to treat everyone as an equal and deal with the situation with a high amount of fairness and compassion.

Aquarius Zodiac Sign

Aquarius is the eleventh zodiac sign. zodiac. It is the sign that covers January 20th through February 18th. The symbol of Aquarius refers to the Water Bearer. It is usually depicted as the figure of a man who pours out water. It is the symbol of changing. The people that are born with the signs of Aquarius are often intelligent, imaginative and self-reliant. In addition, intelligence and wit are an aspect of Aquarian character and Aquarians are more concerned with human beings than riches or possessions. While they're more organised and organized than Gemini however, the Aquarian is equally curious and adventurous. The difference is that most of their adventures are In the mind, whereas Gemini's adventures happen on the outside.

Astrological Aquarius

Aquarius constellation is located in the west. Aquarius constellation is situated within Capricorn to the west, along with Pisces within the eastern. Aquarius is Latin meaning "water (or) cup carrier". Similar to Capricorn it's located in the area of the sky known as the "sea" on due to the water-related constellations, including Pisces the fish and rivers Eridanus along with Cetus The whale.

The Babylonians were believed to have associated Aquarius as The God Ea which was usually depicted as holding a vase that had the water pouring out since this god was the one responsible for the many destructive floods. In the past, in Egypt however the constellation was linked with the annual flood of the Nile and was believed to be the reason Aquarius placed his vase into the river to signal spring's arrival. In Hindu tradition, the constellation is associated with water because it is a symbol of the image of a water pitcher.

According to people of the Greeks, Aquarius was sometimes described as Prometheus Deucalion's son who built a ship along together with Pyrrha his wife to allow them to escape the upcoming flood. They then traveled for nine days before they reached the shore of Mount Parnassus. The Greeks also connect Aquarius with the beautiful Ganymede who was the child of Tros (King of the Trojans). Zeus carried Ganymede on a trip to Mount Olympus to serve as cup bearer to the gods. Another Greek myth connects Aquarius to Cecrops 1, an Athenian ruler who, instead of offering wine, offered sacrificed water to gods.

Aquarius Emotions

Aquarians, however, are also notoriously insecure, lusty and thrive by being different in their thinking and dress style like everyone else, while being accepted enough by people who are around them to be able to relate to them. They have a much easier time trying to get along with people who are just acquaintances as opposed to those supposed to be close to them. The reason is due to the fact that Aquarius individuals are extremely emotional, experiencing all things deeply and not being able to manage their emotions. They cut their emotions out rather than managing them and letting their feelings. This makes them appear quite cold and unfeeling to those close to them. Yet, Aquarius people are very committed and will be with a person until they're confronted with the fact that it's not worth the effort.

Freethinking Aquarians

The Aquarius are full of thoughts and imagination. They're not really children since they aren't as innocent being more intelligent and knowledgeable than the average age. They love technology and are fond of being aware of and using the most recent gadgets. They are also extremely skilled and gifted in their thinking and have an innate love of tinkering. A lot of Aquarius people are inventors, with Thomas Edison being one of them. They have strong opinions, but are willing to change them if they are disproved beyond a shadow of doubt. Otherwise, an Aquarian person will display their indecision, holding the cherished thought or idea with the utmost respect for life.

The Aquarius group loves to fight the flow radical changes, revolutions, and reforms and especially those that be beneficial to the people. Anyone who is born in the

Aquarius sign will not be inclined to pursue wealth, but they'll be practical enough to be able to afford and maintain the necessities of clothing and food, as well as shelter. In terms of money, the majority of Aquarius people fall into the middle class, choosing to focus on causes that are most important to them except when their talents have earned them fortune.

Aquarius at Work

A lot of Aquarius people work in work areas that require forward-thinking whether in science and technology as well as human rights, engineering, or. They are visionaries who have a revolutionary outlook and have a knack for finding ways to solve problems and are able to take advantage of every opportunity that is presented to them and especially those that embrace the new and innovative methods of working. The Aquarius person may undergo a series of career shifts before settling on a permanent position in search of a job that allows the person to grow and share their visions, and carry out their plans in the most complete freedom, most likely within many supportive colleagues.

Ambitions and Aspirations

Since they are free spirits, no one can bind Aquarius people to any beliefs or values they don't like It will not work. A person born in Aquarius is a forward thinker, focusing on their vision of the future and looking for innovative, unique solutions to the various problems faced by the people of the world. With their creativity and resourcefulness, their ability to create ideas so they have the strength and practicality and confidence that they are able to surpass and even break down the bonds that hinder people from achieving their goals, Aquarius people actually have to be careful not to get overly angry or frustrated when they face the possibility of loss in achieving their goals.

The Parental Aquarius

As a parent, an Aquarius person may be a bit lenient with regards to the freedom they grant their children in almost everything they do. While this is beneficial to them as they wish to make their own choices in life, it's certainly not good when Aquarius children come to them with worries and parents want to shield themselves from the stress of being unsure of what to do next after their failed attempts to reduce the children's issues through reasoning.

The Aquarius Child

As a young person, an Aquarius is happy and curious, extremely intelligent and rebellious. This is especially true in their teens. They crave independence and freedom from the earliest age, long before they're ready to be ready. However, their intelligence usually places themselves in the role of the top or the most successful student in class. It is possible that they are not as the most popular students of the teacher however, since Aquarius children usually are elitist in their approach to they believe that work and the class, teacher, or any of them are below their level. But however, the Aquarius child's sociable personality is a popular choice in their group of peers.

Flower Sign...Orchid

The claim to fame "My distinctiveness is what makes me stand out"

Zodiac's orchids are curious and inventive in their designs. It is interesting to note that one may speak without contradiction, but the orchid is aware of what it speaks about.

You're a person with a wide-ranging personality and this could be the reason why people cling at your unique, but not snarky manner of speaking. A orchid looks at the world with a completely different view unlike others. It is quick to come help other people and enjoy solving puzzles throughout every day life. Orchids are strong in keeping order through their obsession with doing the tasks required to be able to function in a day-to-day basis.

These people tend to be a bit different from the norms of thought. They develop their own style to live their lives, and are regarded as intelligent and innovative. Being the Aquarius sign, you should to be thinking about developing your talents in the field of art to attract interest for yourself. In reality, if you're able, you should try to remain connected to your artistic side.

Famous Aquarius Include:

Abraham Lincoln, Alan Alda, Alan Bates, Anna Pavlova, Benny Hill, Bill Maher, Bob Marley, Boris Yeltsin, Bridget Fonda, Burt Reynolds, Charles Darwin, Chris Farley, Chris Rock, Christian Dior, Clare Short, Derek Jarman Denise Richards, Elijah Wood, Eva

Gabor, Franklin D Roosevelt, Galileo Galilei, Geena Davis, George Burns, Ivana Trump, James Deann, John Belushi, John Travolta, John Ruskin, Laura Dern, Lord Byron, Mia Farrow, Nick Hancock, Oliver Reed, Paris Hilton.

AQUARIUS TRAITS

Aquarius Profile Traits
Aquarians are good at communicating when they are on the same page. They love being around like-minded people. If you meet someone who is an Aquarius sign regards you as a friend, he / they will make you feel special and would love to be around your more regularly. As an Aquarian woman or man you are straightforward and straightforward clear and direct and don't mind being a naive and making unneeded changes or adjustments. People around you will be aware of this. It is not your style to let other people exploit your traits, and you're not afraid to express your anger when you're injured or criticized. You tend to make a fuss on your own.

Personally, Aquarians prefer and settle for a calm and peaceful lifestyle. They tend to be very dispassionate and aren't emotional in their relationships. They may choose a relationship which lacks romance, luster and adventure. Aquarius are a smart and intelligent bunch and others tend to be drawn to their minds. They are naturally curious and can pick up things quickly. They are interested in all things around them however, due to this, they often struggle to focus on one thing at a given time.

Aquarius Zodiac Sign

Born between Jan 20-February 18 Aquarius Astrological signs are represented in the zodiac by a pitcher or water bearer. The people born under this symbol of astrology are extremely vulnerable and sensitive. It may appear that they have many acquaintances and friends within their circle however, they actually have a few close and trustworthy friends. It is possible to claim that Aquarians are social people that are not unusual due to the widespread nature of the sign. They enjoy intellectual debates and social interactions as such, which is why you can find them in many groups, forums and clubs.

Aquarius is a sign of the air. Sign

A lot of people think Aquarius as the Water Sign when it is actually an Air Sign. Zodiac signs that belong to the Air Sign are thinkers primarily with their logic and intelligence over their emotions and feelings. They are adept at learning and can effortlessly shift between different ideas. People and women born with this sign have a excellent command of spoken language and are able to express themselves quite easily. That's not to suggest that they don't like to talk however, they will engage in interesting conversations.

Strengths and Positive Qualities

Aquarians are intelligent and talented by their very nature. If they decide to pursue this path they can amaze those around them with their imagination and intelligence they possess. They are also excellent leaders when faced with difficulties and difficult situations. Aquarius appreciate honesty, and while they are prone to think rationally but they also are attuned to their inner senses. They are always asking questions about everything and their unique out-of-the-box perspective on their surroundings provides new perspectives and ideas to other people. Aquarians possess many positive traits, so to say. Their intelligence, versatility, the ability to communicate, and their wit are easy to be noticed. It's not surprising that they create sought-after, great and creative ideas. Despite all the intelligence they possess They are also friendly and compassionate. They are a good and caring people. Aquarius do not neglect the poor and they are known to take the time to engage in human rights initiatives.

Negative Qualities and weaknesses

Aquarians are generally viewed by other people as lonely lovers life, but it's simply because they don't seek out relationships to have one. They're not afraid to spend time finding the one they're looking for. Aquarius signs may also be naggers due to the fact that they seek attention and time from people who are close and close to them. They also tend to get often sick. Because of the negative characteristics in their personal lives the professional lives of their employees is likely to be affected.

Because they can communicate to speak, Aquarians can turn nasty and sarcastic when they criticize others. They're kind, but they can also be a bit dark. Aquarius may be stubborn and will insist that the route they've picked is the right choice. Since they're aloof by nature, they could be so extreme that they appear uncaring and as apathetic to other people. Aquarius may be able to form relationships without feeling the commitment that is typical. According to Aquarius they are also unlikely to have a strong bond to their siblings or parents and could remain distant.

Specific characteristics of Aquarius

Highly intelligent: Aquarians are smart by nature, and are aware of what they like and how they can achieve what they want. They different from others and also their creativity and passion for nature. Because of this, they often get noticed from the crowd.

Innovative: Because they instinctively think differently and dance to the beat of their own drummer, Aquarius tend to churn out new ideas and concepts to tackle problems and issues. If you're feeling stuck You are sure to get a different perspective from your Aquarian companion.

Honesty: Aquarius signs are honest people and in their personal as well as professional lives. They are committed and hard workerswho make sure that they are able to produce high-quality work instead of simply completing the task. This quality makes them stand out and helps them become leaders.

Impulsive: Being impulsive by nature, they are more reactive than they react to, and tend to be first to react before considering the consequences since they are always listening to their intuitions.

Inquisitive: Aquarius's inherent fascination with everything that happens around them could be their greatest friend as well as their biggest foe. This is the reason they're extremely knowledgeable and intelligent at first. However, others might find this trait to be a bit too snooty and annoying.

Aquarius Career

Due to their creative curious, inquisitive and creative nature, Aquarians make good inventors as well as researchers, astronauts, astrologers and scientists. The Aquarius brain has an artistic bent, which makes an exceptional talent in the arts. They are also excellent actors as well as musicians, actresses, and even public performing artists. In addition to being compassionate, everything else, this trait could also help make successful doctors and medical professionals.

You're also very effective when it comes to business situations where your brilliant ideas are utilized However, what is holding you from making greater advancement is your aversion to repetitive day-to-day details. The boredom can cause you to put off tasks.

Aquarius Compatibility

The typical Aquarius has the highest love compatibility to Aries, Gemini, and Libra and is able to work with other Aquarius'sas well as Sagittarius. Aquarius is not fully compatibile to Capricorn, Virgo, Leo and Pisces. Taurus, Cancer, and Scorpio are the only ones that have low compatibility, both in the short-term as well as in the long term. In general, Aquarius is a fairly compatible zodiac sign. Aquarius is also a good match for Cancer. Cancer compatibility is threatened by the unpredictability and the unpredictable nature of Aquarius and Cancer's vulnerability. Aquarius and Taurus The Aquarius is a social person who loves interesting and new things. The Taurus dislikes changes and is content doing the same thing day after day.

Conclusion

Freedom is the life-sustaining aspect of life of Aquarius people. Being an Aquarius you are a person who loves to make people laugh and assist people when they're struggling because of the genuine generosity of your heart, and for this , you do not need or want anything in return. However, you could be misinterpreted as aloof and indifferent by those who aren't aware of your desire for total freedom.

You are also a fan of changes and spontaneity. You might appear uninterested and naive but this is because of your soul's desire to take your own decision and not be influenced by issues and people who can hinder you from experiencing absolute happiness. Life can be stressful with all the rules and dull without enough fresh exciting and intellectually stimulating experiences, and understanding. You are always eager to learn new things and conduct research which allows you to assist others in significant ways.

AQUARIUS COMPATIBILITY

Compatibility Profile

Aquarius is one of the zodiac signs which is nearly as intellectual as Gemini. The main distinction between them are that Aquarius is more traditional and is less inclined to radical concepts. While Gemini are more inclined to be artists the people who are born in Aquarius are more likely to become more technical. However, Aquarius is equally independent and may be more self-sufficient than other signs. It is actually the sign with the highest self-reliance, next to Aries. Aquarius is a great candidate for the sciences and in any field that requires logic. It also means that the idea you propose must be logical. "I believe that it's true because I believe it's real" will not be able to stand up to Aquarius. It is important to be prepared to show your proof. There's a certain paradox in the mind of Aquarians. Don't be shocked by their radically opposing opinions regarding the same topic simultaneously. It doesn't mean that they are confused, it's just that, for Aquarius it is the case that no information can ever be firmly established, and there is always room for improvement and improvement.

Aries with Aquarius

Both are active and independent individuals who appreciate the innovative thinking, forward-looking, and open-minded approach to situations or problems. The synergy between this pair is often vibrant and determined. Both sides have revolutionary ideas and are proud of the freedom of accepted views and beliefs that are being circulated. Aries is more concerned than Aquarius in terms of personal development and is less active in social and community groups. Although they are two distinct people are, the basic goals and perspectives of the two are remarkably similar. In the end, the most important factors in this relationship are the common interests, a shared point of view and social activities.

Emotions of Aries are always fiery. Aquarius is generally the cooler among the two. generally more fair and impartial. If Aries's anger or frustration gets out of control, Aquarius can be the more calm and composed one. Both are energetic and independent. They would like to be free to pursue their own personal desires and interests, and keep them independent of the relationship. The couple allows each other to be independent couples and individuals simultaneously. Aries tends to be the bossy. But, Aries prefers to be treated as an equal and dislikes being controlled. Both signs fight against the authority. They are awestruck by new ideas and are willing to let go of the past to accept new possibilities. They enjoy the thought of challenging tradition and the conventional wisdom. One issue with Aquarius and Aries' compatibility of their relationship is that neither prefers to compromise easily.

Taurus with Aquarius

Taurus tends to take a down-to-earth practical approach to issues in life. Aquarius is more inclined to the forward-thinking approach. This is why the couple frequently diverge on many issues, including politics and social issues with preferences in art, music and reading materials. Aquarius is a follower of the latest trends and is always up to date with the latest happenings in the world as well as the ever-changing fashions. Taurus On contrary, prefers to remain with the traditional with interests that change very little over time, and is more determined. Although the differences in how couples approach their relationship is not likely to cause problems, it might be quite a hassle for those who are.

Taurus is a sign of peace and stability. They're considered to be the creatures of habit. They aren't able to react well to changes regardless of where shift is taking place within their life. Old ways are acceptable for them. The Aquarius has the opposite urge They love changes and seek to be excited. They enjoy the idea of trying something new. In terms of customs and traditions, they're uninterested. Actually, they're typically discontent with the notion. A lot of the fights between them tend to be over this exact subject. Aquarius enjoys to rock the boat. Taurus is not as too keen and is also a bit possessive of their family members, while Aquarius desires independence even in relationships with a commitment. Aquarius is also an ideological person and has a strong opinion about things that are contrary to the common sense and natural wisdom and is something Taurus is unable to comprehend. But, Taurus can help Aquarius in helping Aquarius to become more down to earth, rather than living in the moment.

Gemini with Aquarius

Both significations are distinct who share the same notions and concepts regarding relationship compatibility. The relationship between these two people is unlike any other. They feed off each other and effortlessly bounce ideas back and forward. Both of you are drawn to friendship and scholarly interaction, and with the fusion of Aquarius and Gemini it is the perfect partnership. The best part is that you are able to be wonderful friends as being lovers. The Gemini-Aquarius alliance is valued for their shared interest, interests in social activities and shared views. Every alliance has some challenges. But, these two indicators let the couple use their relationship to overcome the squabbling disagreements.

This couple needs to understand the mental level in order to create a harmonious relationship. Both are looking for someone who enjoys talking about ideas, conversations and discovering. The Aquarius could like or like someone but they need an emotional boost to keep the connection going. They are both open, flexible and often separated. Friendship can develop into a romantic bond and it's possible that you'll look at your feelings towards one another. You both are aware of the way you view relationships. In informal interactions, you are comfortable with each other This is because your character traits of each are comparable.

Cancer in conjunction with Aquarius

Cancer is a sign that Cancer is more tied to nostalgia, domesticity and family more than the Aquarius who is very friendly, but is not as emotionally attached to compatibility. It also tends to have a greater range of interests and tastes. The Cancer is extremely emotional and dependent on familiar settings and prefer living in a single place for extended durations of time. However Aquarius Aquarius is more inclined to take the path that changes with time and will make new friends in a short time and does not require the intimate need that Cancer seeks, allowing them to effortlessly change to new settings. Cancer is worried about financial and material security. They worry in times of uncertainty. Cancer requires Aquarius to provide them with some form of emotional support and bonding, however, this is something they're incapable of.

Both of these symptoms are extremely worried about the other people around them. But it's the Cancer who tends to be more attentive to their family members and those within their immediate surroundings. The Aquarius is more interested in the world and is concerned about the well-being of humans across the globe. They prefer friendship, involvement in the world and social causes, over the devotion to their families. It could make Cancer feel abandoned by their attitude. There are other factors that distinguish this couple:

Cancer is emotionally attached and attached towards their history. They are drawn to familiar places and people , as well as safety. Aquarius however, is a sign of exuberance and is frequently viewed as rebellious. They do not like customs and are averse to their beliefs. Actually Aquarius Aquarius does not mind making major radical modifications to their relationships and their lifestyle.

Leo with Aquarius

Leo's warm personality draws the Aquarius Leo's warmth; Aquarius's intelligence and uniqueness is what draws in the Leo. These signs are quite distinct: Aquarius is a social sign. Friends colleagues, associates and acquaintances are their most important relationships in their lives. Yet, Leo places more importance on their personal relationships. This can be observed in the alliance. Leo believes that the Aquarius as aloof, while Aquarius considers Leo as being over-dramatic and self-absorbed. Although they're different in many ways however, the perspectives and beliefs of both can be very positive.

Leo isn't one to be thought of as a follower. They like to be the centre of attention and look distinct. They're not considered team players due to their determination to make themselves stand out. Aquarius enjoys being a member of groups as well as the local community. They enjoy the camaraderie that is associated with them, even when they aren't the focus of attention. Leo likes control and is an absolute; however, the Aquarius likes to be free and dislikes the dictating character of Leo. Aquarius dislikes the notion of being a slave or domesticated or even in the context of a relationship. It is thought of as fair and cool and impartial; Leo is regarded as being very loyal, self-absorbed and personal. They are often affected by the "treat all people with the same" sensation they experience.

Virgo with Aquarius

These two signs of astrology tackle concepts and issues of compatibility with opposing views However, they maintain an excellent relationship with each other. Virgo is about the details and is a specialist in one particular area often. Aquarius is contrary has a broad stance...not focussing on one particular thing. Virgo is focused on the specific outline of plans, while helping Aquarius Aquarius with implementing their concepts. They make an excellent team for activities that are intellectual or social in the sense of. The team of the two is usually formal, but they are able to show each other love, warm, affection and romantic attraction.

The most significant difference between these two is that Aquarius does not like the authority of others and is averse to traditional values. Aquarius is known to have a passion for excitement and loves to shake things up. Virgo however, in contrast is more careful when it comes to life. They stick to the way that's been tried and tested. They want an orderly life; Aquarius doesn't mind when new developments occur. Virgo is committed to improving their own self-worth, while Aquarius prefers to deal with social development and doesn't want about matters dealing the compatibility of their relationship or feelings.

Libra along with Aquarius

The two signs are very active, actively involved in the community and working in a position that keeps them in contact with the general public. The harmony and compatibility between both makes them excellent companions. Aquarius enjoys being part of social clubs, groups and clubs. Libra is inclined to view Aquarius as more a good friend than a spouse or lover. Libra is an zodiac sign that gives greater attention to the close relationship between two people and this can result in not being an issue or cause of trouble. Both of them are in their minds and are looking for a partner who can keep them in a state of mind and the best part about this pairing is that it is possible to occur in conjunction with one another.

There's not a strong emotional resemblance to this relationship. Both consider their own personal circumstances as detached. Based on shared interest, sharing of ideas , and the intellectual delights they share they both feel content with their bond. They often share their thoughts, mostly in relation to how people should behave to each other, such as equality respect, fairness, and so on. One of the subjects frequently debated is the openness of communication. The most significant difference between Aquarius or Libra is their ideas about relationships. Libras are drawn to romantic love and feel they need an accomplice to be complete. But, Aquarius doesn't enjoy the emotional dependence and a sense of neediness. In addition they possess a rebellion that defies the common wisdom. Libra is about acceptance of others and social behaviour, as well as proper manners.

Scorpio with Aquarius

Scorpio people tend to trust their instincts, while those of Aquarius sign tend to be more rational. Aquarius sign are thought of as idealistic and often astonished by the powerful emotional reactions of Scorpio as well as illogical hatreds and love. The truth is, people of the Aquarius sign are more sensible. Scorpio however, may get smitten with one person and become emotionally attached to their partner, while Aquarius is aloof and distant and enjoys having many acquaintances and friends, but isn't a fan of the connection that other signs enjoy. This is why there is a gap in emotions among Scorpio and Aquarius that is difficult to overcome. Both signs do not hesitate to share their opinion, and sometimes tend to be stubborn about it. If you want this partnership to be successful you need to be aware of the different perspectives and be able to recognize them.

The needs for emotional support of the two are incredibly different, and can cause problems if there's a mutual understanding and acceptance between the two. Since Aquarius as well as the Scorpio are firmly anchored in their beliefs, they aren't necessarily open to the notion of change unless it's according to their own terms. Scorpios need emotional intimacy and intimacy due to that they can be highly jealous and manipulative trying to control others' emotions. Aquarius isn't a fan of possessiveness in Scorpios due to their fierce independence. Additionally, since they let their emotions go free, they may be obsessed with their desires. But they are also the Aquarius person tends to be aloof when they are dealing with feelings and emotions. In reality, Aquarius might feel there is no understanding of the intense emotional reaction of Scorpio towards their love affair.

Sagittarius is paired with Aquarius

Both Aquarius and Sagittarius are outgoing and have active lifestyles that keep them on their toes. Both are fond of making new friends and staying on top of current news, including literature and music, the arts and politics. Sagittarius is a bit more philosophical than Aquarius and is a fan of having a reason or purpose to their relationships. In reality, they're at risk of being sucked into overly-excited visions and fantasies. The only issue for this couple is that not romantic and often disengaged. But for they, this is perfectly fine! Both are fiercely independent which is good since this means that they each have their own freedom and space. While their tastes are different, they are able to be combined to create an engaging, fun and incredibly satisfying relationship.

The reason why the Aquarius as well as the Sagittarius pair is due to the fact that their emotional and mental desires are similar to one another. Both are independent and have a an intense desire to encounter things that are unfamiliar to them. Both are able to adapt to changes quite easily, and will often look for a change whenever things become dull or there isn't a problem. Both Sagittarius or Aquarius prefer domesticity, and both prefer being part of people from all walks of life (a network of social contacts). Both believe that their respect for one another and their freedom and happiness are the most essential elements in a relationship that is successful and do not like being directed to do something or any kind of jealousy. Both love the unique styles that defy tradition to have fun.

Capricorn with Aquarius
The couple spends the majority of their time working as well as their careers, so their talents and interests are often in sync with each other. They both contribute to and compatibility. Capricorn provides impartiality, reliability determination, sanity and a level of focus. Aquarius is a sensitive to current problems, imagination, increased awareness of the complexities and the ability to communicate with several people. The issue with this relationship is that the

focus is given to matters other than the relationship. It's therefore not unusual for them to be separated from each other. There are astrological influences that could give the partnership an emotional sensitivity, warm and an attraction.

Both of these signs typically are at odds with their feelings and needs. Aquarius their independence often sees them rejecting the conventional wisdom of society, society and even authority people. They usually want to step away from established methods and pursue something completely different. Capricorns tend to stick with tradition and are generally cautious when they are involved in the unexplored. They're thought of as conservatives and respect things that have been proven to be right. Even when they're philosophically liberal they're still prudent by nature, so they're less likely to take risks. Aquarius loves their freedom. Aquarius enjoys their freedom , and will never be at home. Capricorn is, however, a lover of the concept of commitment, but isn't able to fully comprehend the liberated nature of Aquarius. Both aren't comfortable showing their emotions in their relationships.

Aquarius is associated with Aquarius

The Aquarius couple that is the same sign are very active and outgoing when they reside in an urban area They're unlikely to be in the house a lot. The couple is likely to work for larger companies and organisations. They both are adamant and up to date with the latest developments in politics, art, and science. They have similar interests in the field of science and technology and have an excellent psychological compatibility which is crucial to their respective. It could appear that the couple are friendly but their relationship could lack a sense of depth and sensitivity. Many Aquarius couples are unsure whether they're really couples or just friends. Both Aquarius do not want to be controlled and they are adamant about their individuality. It is not uncommon to be rebellious in the game of the couple from this zodiac sign.

The most important thing for both of them is being an integral part of something larger than them, such as an organization, group or organization. In reality, they find themselves part of a larger circle of friends, if not with the entire world. Aquarius Aquarius isn't comfortable accepting the behavior of others, particularly when it isn't in line with their beliefs. It can be difficult in accepting their own feelings and actions, especially when they're not noble and fair. Both parties are in a state of disconnection from what they feel and tend to ignore other people's struggles. Because of this, many think of the Aquarius as distant and cold. The Aquarius couple is usually good companions and respects their beliefs and visions. However, there is sometimes a lackluster spark in the romantic aspect in the marriage.

Pisces along with Aquarius

It is believed that Pisces as well as Aquarius tend to have an open mind and are open to new ideas, particularly when they're innovative. The Aquarius is more logical than Pisces who are guided by their intuition and emotions. Pisces often struggle to express their thoughts and values , while the Aquarius can offer excellent arguments for their opinions or positions. Pisces is a person who is sympathetic and can sense the pain and wants. While Aquarius is a compassionate approach to life, they are more concerned with principles and ideals rather than people and their struggles and are able to separate emotions while ensuring objectivity. Pisces however, on however, are unable to accomplish this as they seek intimacy and emotional connection more than their Aquarius partners can usually handle or even offer. Actually it is said that the Aquarius does not like dependency or emotionally overly sensitive people.

The personalities of these two differ significantly. Pisces is considered to be a peace-loving, non-competitive and naturally gentle. They are enthralled by the idea of being away from the world for a while. Aquarius enjoys being involved in their surroundings, and prefers to stay "in in the flow" of everything. Pisces is psychically and emotionally sensitive, which is a sign that has extremely deep emotions. Aquarius is, on the contrary side, appears to be sensible and savvy to the circumstances and individuals. However, while they do possess an instinct for helping others around the

Aquarius, Aquarius doesn't appear to be compassionate, as opposed to Pisces who many use to their advantage. Pisces generally don't appreciate the cool and detached character of Aquarius who prefers to seek out intellectual stimulation instead of the emotions that Pisces frequently displays in their relationships.

Chapter 9: Aquarius Friendship

Friendship Profile

Aquarius governs Aquarius is the ruler of Eleventh House of Friends which is not surprising that they seem as if they are friends with everybody. It's not a good idea to believe these rumors until you attempt to meet the water Bearer However. While they're known to many people, Aquarius rarely lets people meet their personalities on a personal scale. They're a bit distant in regards to their real emotions. If you're ever feeling down however, Aquarius will jump at the chance to purchase dinner or anything else to be exact. They're not trying to purchase your friendship. Why would they?

However, they are extremely generous and willing to assist those in need. Do not let this turn you overly clingy. If you're an Aquarian is worried about the loss of independence, or they feel like they're in a secluded place by their surroundings, they're likely to create an attempt to break the door. The water Bearer has a sense of adventure. Make sure you keep an open mind and they'll lead you to interesting new locations. The ideal Aquarius friend is someone with whom they have connections that are intellectual. If you allow them to have their space and keep the conversation going and engaging, they'll become your best friend for the rest of your life.

Best Friend Bets: Sagittarius, Aries

Aries and Aquarius

If Aries and Aquarius create a bond and a partnership, the mixture of Aquarian vision and Aries actions tends to make the two a highly creative team. Their bond is not static. And, although it may be fierce, it's never dull! This couple can be wonderful partners; their personalities are different which tends to be a good match and enable them to get along. Both of them are optimistic and enthusiastic about their lives and, together, they relish exciting and new adventures. They both are drawn to everything new and are both thrill seekers. They may even play the show!

Aries-Aquarius friendships often have the feeling of admiration and respect for one another. Aries is awed by the originality of vision, creativity and inventiveness that are that is characteristic of Aquarius. The reverse is also true. Aquarius appreciates Aries enthusiasm and determination. Aquarians always have fresh ideas however they may not always have the energy to execute them in as Aries does. Both love their independence However, conflicts may arise when Aries appears to be too dominant of their space or Aquarius appears too distant or disengaged. The two friends need to realize that they perceive the world differently. Aries may be too involved with Aquarius tastes as well as Aquarius could, in turn could be too unpredictably for their Aries companion.

Aries is an astrological sign that is ruled by Planet Mars Aries is ruled by Mars, while Aquarius is controlled by the planets Saturn as well as Uranus. The three Planets make up a cycle that speaks to the Aries-Aquarius alliance and their capability to come together to bring about major change. Uranus can be described as the Planet of innovative ideas and creative thinking and it's the Uranus Planet that Aquarius is able to get its brilliant vision. Mars implements these ideas into action and takes actions. Then, Saturn keeps the process running until it is completed, following the steps after Uranus's enthusiasm has waned as Mars' energy shifts to new ideas.

Aries is the Fire Sign. They are ablaze with energy It's very rare for one to become tired and the other to keep going. Even though they can disagree frequently but their disagreements aren't lasting long. They're not too focused on the next challenge to keep an unresolved grudge! There may, occasionally there will be a struggle for supremacy, and compromise will be required. If these two keep their egos under control and keep their egos in check, it'll be a smooth ride.

Aries is known as the Cardinal Sign. When you have an Aries-Aries pairing each partner is adept at starting things which is why they don't spend time trying to figure out what they are doing before they dive to something using all their energy. If they know the outcome they desire, they head to it! The greatest thing about the Aries-Aries relationship is the lively, spontaneous character of their energy. The two friends will never be bored! Their energy and their ability to resolve disagreements creates a fiery but also a mutually beneficial relationship.

Taurus and Aquarius

If Taurus and Aquarius create a bond and move mountains together, they will be able to do so. Taurus is practical and has a simple approach to living. Aquarius has an unusual way of thinking about all things! It may seem like they share some common interests, however, they have a strong determination to achieve. When these two forces are in sync and work together, they will succeed at almost anything.

Each Taurus and Aquarius can be adamant and vocal. They are both known for doing things the way they want to without fuss or fuss as feasible. Taurus likes routine and is a conservative. Aquarius has a modern outlook and is bored and boring. Taurus is likely to find Aquarius thrilling, but might be frustrated in trying to get into this creator's mind. Aquarius does not like the domineering nature of Bulls. Bull but will find the solid foundation Taurus offers as an ideal support, though they might not agree to it.

Taurus is the sign of Venus and Aquarius is controlled by Saturn and Uranus. Venus is an energy of feminine warmth and Saturn is a cold and masculine energy. Uranus is all about things odd and bizarre. Venus is about love and physicality and both are significant to Taurus. Saturn is all about hard work and discipline to reach goals as Uranus is a symbol of forward-thinking. Taurus will teach Aquarius the fact that living is built on emotions, and is enhanced through beauty and comfort. Aquarius will teach Taurus to remain more detached and continue to reach to get what it wants and to get away from things if they aren't effective.

Taurus can be described as an Earth Sign, and Aquarius is an Air Sign. Aquarius is a sign of pure intellectual exploration, whereas Taurus can be more practical. Taurus asks: 'how can this aid me in reaching what I want to achieve in this life What can I do to help me achieve my goals?' While Aquarians just look at what is interesting to them whether it's practical as well, but often inquire "what else?" Sometimes, these friends might have difficulty comprehending where the other trying to communicate with. It is possible to have conflicts in this type of relationship when Taurus is too demanding or Aquarius appears distant and cold. Both parties must be taught how they see the world differently.

Taurus And Aquarius Are both fixed Signs that are both Fixed. They share an incredibly strong will and perseverance when working towards the target. If they are able to establish a plan and stick to it until they get the results. So, if everyone is committed to their friendship and trusts each other, their bond will be strong. If they disagree on a particular idea however, they could be in perpetual disagreement. Taurus will not change their minds because they view it as the result of their control and character and Aquarius might view Taurus as too rigid boring and dull. If they understand that cooperation can be more productive than banging heads, they'll stay productive. Taurus is more stoic than Aquarius However, they could, in a certain degree accept a compromise to avoid the whole war, if it's sensible to do this.

The most appealing aspect of the Taurus-Aquarius bond is that once they decide to join forces, they're an unstoppable duo. Both are extremely powerful individuals and neither can take on the other regardless of how difficult they attempt! When they can overcome their differences, and come together and be able to agree on their own individuality and values, their partnership can be fantastic!

Gemini and Aquarius

If Gemini and Aquarius make a connection and they are able to enjoy an amazing connection to the mind.

Aquarius is a visionary that attracts Gemini who appreciates the merits of a great idea or idea. Both are a bit of an independent pair. Arguments could arise when Aquarius is irritated by Gemini's tendency towards dithering or when Gemini believes that Aquarius is too inflexible. They're well-matched. Aquarius will adopt the necessary steps to make the alliance's objectives into reality and Gemini will be fully in the support of Aquarius the actions of Aquarius. When this pair is able to concentrate its energies and focus it, it will be able to accomplish whatever goal it is, no matter how vast.

The two Gemini and Aquarius are full of energy. By having a chat, they can develop amazing ideas and goals that are common to both. The two Sign is one to be idle! Aquarius loves to dive into their biggest thoughts and plot their next steps. Gemini likes intellectual freedom and can consider every aspect of an argument, and also see the reasons behind the Aquarian's decisions. If Gemini is in a state of flux, Aquarius can help stabilize their actions, but they must also be cautious to give Gemini time to think, and not become too overwhelming.

Aquarius is controlled by the Planets Saturn and Uranus as well as Gemini is managed by Mercury, the Planet Mercury.

These Planets symbolize communication and the ability to see things from a different perspective, and, especially for Aquarius and Gemini, the ability to stay focused after an action plan has been implemented. Due to this, Aquarius and Gemini are able to work together They are both adept in the art of making plans. If there is a lively exchange taking place between the two

Signs It will be more likely to be for enjoyment and intellectual challenges of it.

Each Aquarius along with Gemini are both air signs. The dual nature of the two signs fuels their intellect relationship and keeps it growing. Gemini is awed by the innovative energy and the sociable nature of the Aquarius Water Bearer. Aquarius is able to develop ideas that spark Gemini's curiosity and enthusiasm. Gemini can follow the example of Aquarius and get involved in any of their quick-witted friends' numerous plans, while maintaining an eye for the intellectual. Both Signs have a wide range of interests and Gemini's desire to research and think provides them with plenty of material for lively discussion.

Gemini is an Mutable Sign Gemini is a Mutable Sign. Aquarius is a fixed Sign. Aquarius is the one who sees the future of the Zodiac filled with great ideas. Gemini will embrace these concepts and play around for hours with Aquarius! If they are spending time together, they will not debate who should claim the credit for their thoughts and experiences. The relationship will be more successful when Gemini lets Aquarius to take over the leadership.

The greatest benefit of the Gemini-Aquarius relationship is their ability to combine their energies and make use of their unique talents to achieve any goals they have decide to set for themselves. Together, they are able to be a source of inspiration to each other's ideas and fancies. Their conversational skills are a success, which makes their friendship healthy.

Cancer and Aquarius

If Cancer and Aquarius create a bond this could be a drawing between two opposite extremes in the spectrum. Cancer is a person with an emotional outlook on life. Aquarius has an unconventional unorthodox approach to nearly every circumstance. While Cancer might hide away, Aquarius is the gregarious host in the friends group and excels in social and business situations. If they can both be able to unite their strengths positively and work well together, they'll be able to travel the world together.

Both Cancer as well as Aquarius are both driven and ambitious. They prefer to live life in their own way, and aren't averse to face resistance. Cancer is a fan of the old-fashioned and traditional and displays the morality of a conservative. Aquarius is modern and overwhelmed by routine, the boring and dull. Cancer is likely to find Aquarius fascinating, but may be overwhelmed trying to get into the revolutionary's mind. Aquarius won't enjoy the power of a prickling Crab however they will appreciate the solid foundation Cancer can offer to be an excellent source of helper. They'll just have for it to be known!

Cancer is controlled by the Moon and Aquarius is the sign of Saturn as well as Uranus. It is believed that the Moon is a bright feminine energy, and Saturn is an icy, masculine energy. Uranus is about everything strange and unique. It is a sign of the Moon is emotional and concerned with domesticity and growth, and both are crucial to Cancer. Saturn is about work and discipline to reach objectives, while Uranus represents forward-thinking. Cancer can teach Aquarius to make decisions based on emotions. Aquarius could teach Cancer to become better at separating themselves, free them from situations that are uncontrollable and to reevaluate their goals if they're off track.

Cancer is an Water Sign, and Aquarius is an Air Sign. Aquarius is a person who lives life with a pure and intellectual research, while Cancer is more practical. Cancer asks, "How do you feel how do you feel?' while Aquarians just pay attention to their interests and ask , 'what else do you want to know? The Aquarians might find it difficult to comprehend the other's source of thinking. There can be conflicts in this type of friendship when Cancer is demanding, or Aquarius is too cool and refuses Cancer emotional comfort. Both should be aware that they see the world differently and should be able to celebrate their differences instead of feeling threatened.

Cancer is one of the Cardinal Sign, while Aquarius is an Fixed Sign. Both are inclined to persist in pursuing their objectives. If they've got a defined course, they'll stick to it until the finish. Once they've made that spending time with each other is worthwhile, they'll not be able to shake off this belief. If they disagree They may discover that Cancer has the most determined or more rigid partner, who isn't averse to the influence of emotions. Aquarius might view Cancer as too emotional. If they know they're working in an admiration and respect for each other, then it's easier to be friends.

The greatest benefit of the Cancer-Aquarius relationship is that when the pair decides to join forces, they can be a formidable force. If they can resolve their differences, join forces and establish the core functioning of their relationship and the dynamics of their relationship can create a positive equilibrium.

Leo and Aquarius

In the event that Leo and Aquarius create a bond and a partnership, the mixture between Aquarian insight and Leo imagination is enough to make the world pay attention. This relationship is energetic and energetic, and even though occasionally, there may be competition between them, there's no dull moment for the two! They make excellent business partners and friends Their personalities are friendly and they have a great connection. Both are optimistic and enthusiastic about their lives. Both are attracted by things that are new and enjoy thrills. They might sometimes turn their lives into a huge challenge that is called Truth or Dare.

Many relationships between Leo and Aquarius thrive by mutual respect. Leo appreciates the distinctiveness, vision, and creative traits of Aquarius. It is in turn, Aquarius appreciates the Lion's strength charisma and dignity. Aquarians always have fresh ideas however they may not always have the courage to make ideas a reality in the same manner that Leo does. Both are a bit of an independent however, conflict can occur in the event that Leo appears too dominant or Aquarius appears too distant or distant. The two friends must discover that they perceive the world differently. Leo is often too exuberant for Aquarius tastes, but Aquarius is, on the other hand could be uncertain for their Leo friend. If they can communicate to one another the value of their friendship, everything will be okay!

Leo is guided by Leo is ruled by the Sun Leo is ruled by the Sun, while Aquarius is controlled by Planets Saturn as well as

Uranus. The three Planets make up a cycle that is a reflection of the Leo-Aquarius relationship and their ability to join forces to form new institutions. Uranus represents the Planet of fresh ideas and creative thinking. It's the Uranus Planet that Aquarius receives its visionary ideas. Then , the Sun brings life and identity to their concepts. Then, Saturn keeps things moving until they are completed and follows the steps after Uranus' inspiration is exhausting and sun's energies been diverted to new ideas.

Leo is an Fire Sign, and Aquarius is an Air Sign. Air creates Fire as well as keeps it running; Aquarius can keep up with the energy and action of Leo and make unique effects using the control panel, making Leo the Lion shine like a star. They are able to reach incredible heights. Aquarius is able to utilize the power of intellect to stimulate Leo's desire and provide new ideas to apply and are very stimulating for Leo. Together, they create an upward spiral of personal development and growth. They share a wide range of interests and Leo's drive to contribute to the world allows them to implement the ideas of Aquarius, who is more reserved. Aquarius.

Leo as well as Aquarius Both are Fixed signs. Leo is the sign that gives Aquarius the courage to move ahead and get involved instead of being in the lab of a mad scientist creating new concepts. Aquarius will surprise their Leo acquaintances with their unique vision and their uniqueness. They are dedicated and loyal and, when they realize that they don't have to be the one to lead or to follow to succeed, they will be successful as a group.

The most appealing aspect of Leo and Aquarius's friendship is the ability they have to accomplish so much when they are together. This is not a sedate couple! Fixed Fire and Fixed Air cover all points, they can think of a great idea, then figure out the best way to implement it and then stick to it in order to achieve success. The whole process makes it an alliance of vision as well as the ability to take action.

Virgo and Aquarius

If Virgo and Aquarius make a connection and a relationship, it's an issue of two people bring out the best and the worst of each other. Virgo has a more conventional method of living that is scientific. The Aquarian approach is, however is a radical departure from all boundaries of science. The two may be able to thrive on their differences, however, they develop when they get to know one another. Aquarius is unpredictable and impulsive, while Virgo prefers to approach things efficiently and with as little effort as it is possible. Virgo likes order and has a calm, steady mind. Aquarius is contemporary and is bored and boring. Virgo finds Aquarius thrilling, however, they could be frustrated in trying to understand the artist's mind. Aquarius does not like the criticisms of their companion, but will appreciate the strong base Virgo can provide to be an excellent helper.

Virgo is the sign of Mercury and Aquarius is the astrological sign of Saturn along with Uranus. The two Mercury as well as Uranus are energetically androgynous, while Saturn is an energetic, cool and traditional energy. Uranus is all about things unusual and unusual. Mercury is a communicator and is focused on efficiency and organization and all of these are essential to Virgo. Saturn is about work and discipline to reach goals and goals, while Uranus is focused on forward-thinking. Virgo will teach Aquarius that their lives are based on order, logic and the feeling of comfort. Aquarius could teach Virgo to be more distant and even to dig into and defend what they believe in.

Virgo has been identified as one of the Earth Sign, and Aquarius is an Air Sign. Aquarius travels through life in search of an intellectual thrill, whereas Virgo tends to be more pragmatic. Virgos look for the "why" and "how" of an event, whereas Aquarians focus on what entices them whether it's practical or not, and often ask, 'What's is next is next? Sometimes, the two partners might be unable to comprehend the other's viewpoint. There can be conflicts in this relationship if Virgo's attention is on the perfect state or Aquarius appears to be too unpredictable and distant. Both partners must be aware that they see the world from different perspectives and have much to learn from each other.

Virgo is a mutable Sign It is also a Fixed Sign. Aquarius is a fixed Sign. Aquarius can be irritable or opinionated, and is also rigid. Everyone who is a friend works towards an end. Virgo can adapt to any circumstance. Virgo is happy to assist with their Aquarian partner with all idea they have in mind, so it is clear that they are valuable and a vital part of the team. Conflicts are rare and few from being resolved, but they are usually solved through Virgo's friendly nature. If both sides realize they're part of the same team and are in the same boat, it's easier to achieve it. Virgo is more pragmatic than Aquarius and could at times accept a compromise to avoid a full-on conflict when it's practical. The greatest benefit of the friendship between Aquarius and Virgo is that, when they decide to get together they're an ambitious couple. Their relationship can be enriching and pure joy for both.

Libra and Aquarius

In the event that Libra and Aquarius create a friendship The relationship increases the power and awareness of both parties. The relationship is largely without stagnation. Aquarius and Libra have a common love for the arts and dislike limits in their lives.

Aquarius is a more active learner, whereas Libra is content with reading a good book. Together, they'll discover things that they may not have noticed prior to. They both Aquarius and Libra are full of energy! When they get together, they develop amazing ideas and realize that they have several goals in common. Aquarius enjoys having the freedom to play around with various concepts. Libra likes intellectual independence and is able to examine every side of the debate and understand Aquarius often have difficult-to-deduce motives behind their individual decisions. If Libra is unsure, Aquarius can help them determine their position. Libra is adept of smoothing the feathers of the Water Bearer, the idealistic one.

Libra is the home of Planet Venus, and Aquarius is ruled by the planets Uranus as well as Saturn. These Planets symbolize the pleasure of radical vision and, in particular for Aquarius they have the capability to make enemies suffer. This is because Aquarius and Libra collaborate well as a team. They are proficient in achieving their goals accomplished in various ways. They can also argue about things, however, Libra swiftly stifles any outbursts of anger that result from Aquarius constantly flirting. They're a formidable pair particularly when they stand up for social justice and radical changes in the community.

Each Libra along with Aquarius are air signs. The strong emotional and intellectual bonds maintain them. Libra and Aquarius have a common tendency to meet and take part in the new ventures that Libra initiates. If they cooperate, anything is possible! Libra follows the Aquarian guide and get involved in any of their plans with an intellectual perspective. Both are interested in a variety of things and Libra's need to examine and keep the harmony in place is a source of inspiration for many discussions.

Libra is an Cardinal Sign, while Aquarius is Fixed Sign. Aquarius is known as the social mother hen , and also the genesis of ideas that are iconoclastic and Libra can accept these concepts provided they don't feel pressured into it. When they're with each other, they don't argue over who gets responsibility for the achievements or adventure. They don't get caught up in who's getting the most attention or who's working in the background.

The greatest benefit of the Libra-Aquarius relationship is their ability to work as in a group. Together they are able to learn more than they could on their own. Their successes and friendship make for a great and extremely successful friendship.

Scorpio and Aquarius

In the event that Scorpio and Aquarius create a bond that is a mix of diverse needs and different views. Scorpio is a fiery personality and a way of dealing with their daily lives. Aquarius is a unique perspective on the world, which is idealistic. While Scorpio might be more reserved and prefer working alone, Aquarius enjoys socializing with other people. They might appear to share some common interests, but they both are possessed of a strong willpower. If they can commit this effort to achieve a shared objective, they can be sure of success and enjoyment.

The two Scorpio and Aquarius can be very difficult and highly opinionated. They are the type of people who like things in as they want them without question. Scorpio is a shrewd, discerning soul who digs deep into the significance of the things. Aquarius can be modern, and doesn't like attention to detail. Scorpio is likely to find Aquarius thrilling, however, they might be frustrated when trying to break into the mind of this revolutionary. Aquarius isn't awed by the prickly nature of a Scorpion or the level of attention they demand However, they will appreciate the determination Scorpio offers to be an excellent source of support.

Scorpio is controlled by The Planets Mars as well as Pluto and Aquarius is the sign of Saturn as well as Uranus. Mars is a powerful violent, belligerent and courageous masculine energy and Pluto stimulates these impulses and provides a rebirthing circular nature. Saturn is an energy that is cool and contained and Uranus is all about everything extraordinary and unique. Mars is emotional and reacts without taking things into consideration; that is the character of Scorpio. In the case of Aquarius, Saturn is about determination and hard work to accomplish goals. Uranus influences thinking ahead. Scorpio can teach Aquarius about living that is based on emotions and how to look beneath the surface. Aquarius could teach Scorpio to be more distant and detached from circumstances that can be a challenge and review their goals when they're not on the right track.

Scorpio is an Water Sign, and Aquarius is an Air Sign. Aquarius is a person who lives life with an unrelenting, creative exploration, whereas Scorpio is more structured. Scorpio seeks out purpose while Aquarius is looking for the exciting. Both of them might have trouble finding out where the other's ideas originate. The two could get into a fight when Scorpio seems too domineering or Aquarius appears too cool and smug and is unable to offer Scorpio assurance. Both partners must learn that they perceive the world differently and they ought to be happy and be jolly about their differences.

Scorpio as well as Aquarius Both are Fixed signs. Both are stubborn, solitary and uncompromising. Both of them tend to stay focused when working towards an end. If they've got a strategy and stick to it, they'll do so until they're successful. When they've made their minds that they will achieve things together, they'll never lose hope of maintaining their friendship. If they are of different opinions and opinions, they might discover they are one of them, the Scorpion will be the persistent and more rigid companion. If both of them consider the benefits of their connection They will be in a position to overcome any differences they face.

The most appealing aspect of the Scorpio-Aquarius partnership is their capacity to win and glory when they work together. Both have extremely strong personalities So neither will be able to overpower one another. When they are able to work some differences out, join together and be able to agree on their own individuality The fruits of their friendship will be delicious.

Sagittarius and Aquarius

If Sagittarius and Aquarius make a connection The mixture of Aquarian vision and Sagittarian expertise makes an extremely creative and unique pair. This pair is unbound by restrictions, and though it is fierce, it's never boring! They are great companions; their personalities are in a different direction and this can be a good match and enable them to get along. Both are optimistic and passionate about their lives together, and they love laughter and fun. They can fly together without the fear of falling.

A lot of Sagittarius-Aquarius friendships have the feeling of admiration and respect for one another. Sagittarius is awed by the singularity, vision, and creativity that are typical of Aquarius. The reverse is also true. Aquarius is awed by the Sagittarian creativity and brilliance. Sagittarius always has fresh ideas however they may not always have the energy to execute them like Aquarius does. Both are independent and freedom, and there aren't any disagreements because this is the perfect combination for them both. There are times when Sagittarius might appear too indulgent for Aquarius which could as a result might be too odd for their Sagittarian companion. So long as they're transparent about their positive feelings regarding their relationship, they'll be able to overcome negative feelings.

Sagittarius is ruled by the planet Jupiter and Aquarius is directed by the planets Saturn as well as Uranus. The three Planets create a cycle that shows the compatibility between Sagittarius and Aquarius as well as their capacity to develop and nurture each other. Uranus can be described as being the Planet of fresh ideas and creative thinking. It's that from the Planet that Aquarius receives its unique perspective. Jupiter is the one to help by influencing the way to greater learning, growth and prosperity. In the end, Saturn keeps these friends going forward with their plans until they're completed and follows up on Uranus's inspiration was exhausted and Jupiter's energies move into new directions.

Sagittarius is one of the Fire Sign, and Aquarius is an Air Sign. Air fuels fire and keeps it burning. Then, Fire is powered by the power of Air. Sagittarius is capable of keeping in line with Water Bearer's desire to create a variety of experiments that are based on the latest ideas. If they are spending time together, they make an intriguing, imaginative couple! Aquarius and Sagittarius make use of their intellect and curiosity to generate the mind with new ideas, and they also encourage their respective creativity. Both are avid readers and Sagittarius is a person who wants to be physically active is a major factor in using the ideas of fast-witted Aquarius into the real world.

Sagittarius is an Mutable Sign while Aquarius is a fixed Sign. Sagittarius can effortlessly play with the odds and is always willing to start or stop whatever plans the two may have. Aquarius is somewhat less tolerant but is willing to see any plan remain in motion so long as they're determined to see it through. Aquarius helps to stabilize and finish projects instead of taking on new projects without having completed the previous ones while Sagittarius likes to move from one task to the next as their mood dictates. Both are loyal dedicated to one another, and they are able to do a lot.

The greatest thing about the friendship between Sagittarius and Aquarius is the ability to accomplish many things while they're together. Mutable Fire and Fixed Air provide all the necessary information They can both come out with an idea then work out the best way to make it happen and then stick with it until it is fully realized. Their formidable partnership creates a partnership of motion and flexibility.

Capricorn and Aquarius

If Capricorn and Aquarius make a connection It is an alliance between two individuals who can bring out the best in one another. Capricorn is a cautious, practical attitude to living. Aquarius is a ferocious visionary outlook on all things! They might appear to be completely opposites, but once they decide to pursue an identical purpose, they're unstoppable.

The two Capricorn and Aquarius are both indecisive and possessive. Capricorn enjoys the organization aspect and always seeking outcomes. Aquarius is an affluent and modern person and finds boring routines that are dull and boring. Capricorn is likely to find Aquarius thrilling, however, they could be frustrated in trying to discover a sensible order in their delusional mysterious mind. Aquarius do not like the dominant nature of their friend however they will find the solid base Capricorn offers as a wonderful assistance. They will be glad that someone else will be able to take care of their common needs and interests.

Capricorn as well as Aquarius are both ruled by Saturn as well as Aquarius is also controlled by Uranus. Saturn is an energetic, cool and traditional energy. It is a planet that is focused and committed to the development of thinking. Capricorn and Aquarius combine their strengths and contribute to Aquarian revolutionary movements as well as Capricorn the social standing. Uranus is all about things unique and different. Capricorn will teach Aquarius how life can be built on order, logic and the comfort of. Aquarius can inspire Capricorn to dream bigger and be more assertive about what they believe in.

Capricorn can be described as one of the Earth Sign, and Aquarius is an Air Sign. Aquarius is a person who lives life with the pursuit of pure and uninvolved exploration, while Capricorn seeks an end product. Sometimes, these two friends may be unable to comprehend the other's viewpoint. It is possible to have conflicts within this group of friends in the event that Capricorn is too focussed or Aquarius is too distracted by their own lives and goals. Both must learn how to navigate their paths in different ways and have plenty of things to offer one another.

Capricorn is an Cardinal Sign, while Aquarius is fixed sign. Both are incredibly indecisive and uncompromising. They tend to pursue issues with a relentless focus. If they've got a plan and stick to it, they'll follow it until they've got the outcome they desire from the circumstance. Capricorn prefers to come up with plans and distribute the responsibility. Aquarius is happy to work with Capricorn when they are given a major part. Conflicts could arise because of the arrogance that both significations have. But, if they know they're a part of a group due to shared tastes and a mutual respect and admiration it's much more easy for them to reach a harmonious balance.

The most appealing aspect of the Capricorn-Aquarius relationship can be that when the two decide to get together, they form an unbreakable pair. The friendship will be enriching and enjoyable for both parties. The bond they share will be a benefit to them as well as their friends' circle.

Aquarius and Aquarius

When two Aquarians make a connection they think about the common good of all humanity. The two are intent on making new acquaintances, helping others and advocating for change in society. They are lively and social and enjoy themselves even when they're in the middle of it all. They get along well, and may even cause occasional sighs and minor jealousies of their fellow colleagues. They enjoy keeping up with current events and implementing contemporary, innovative concepts.

Individual and cosmopolitan. All of their social interactions can cause them to feel emotional detached. They are primarily focused on external, and they perform effectively both independently and in a larger group, such as an event, group or group. Sometimes, the pair is a bit difficult to confront the truth about their feelings, whether they are their ownor their friends' or those around them. They have an idea of what people should be doing that is more frequently than not an un-personal perspective.

Aquarius is it is ruled by Planets Saturn as well as Uranus. Uranus is the planet that controls innovative or radical concepts. They are always reaching out with their visionary outlook and visions, the Aquarian intelligence is so extreme and wild that Aquarius is often referred to for being the Einstein of the Zodiac. They are a part of a group of people who have ideas that are too out of the ordinary to all of humanity and are often dismissed as skeptics. But, Saturn contains a great attitude to work, determination and responsibility. It also guides the Aquarian members to be adamant for what they desire. This makes the friendship extremely productive and highly respected.

Aquarius is an Air Sign. The ability to think and tackle issues using their exceptional intellect is a natural part of their lives. The same drive to think that makes Aquarian team members self-assured and confident is also the cause of the physical or emotional disconnect the pair may experience. They're a fantastic group and can be a wonderful conversations, however the various aspects of their relationship can require an enormous amount of work and energy. They can also become cold to people that they consider boring and insignificant.

Aquarius is a fixed Sign. Their fixed nature can make this couple extremely productive as well as incredibly stubborn. Ideas come from the Aquarius imaginative mind, and both partners have an appreciation for each other's contribution to a common objective. However, there are times when their opinions can clash, and result in disagreement. Both friends share the same dislike and distaste for people who don't share the desire to progress.

The greatest benefit of the Aquarius-Aquarius connection is that they are able to bring fresh ideas and institutional structures into the global. As visionaries and as individuals the duo take an initiative for positive change in culture and innovative ideas. So long as the two friends keep in mind to include a touch of humor, the relationship can be a huge contribution to the community as well as all the people that are involved.

Pisces and Aquarius

If Aquarius and Pisces make a connection it's a matter of love and creativity. The two friends are idealistic as individuals and in a group. Pisces has a flow that is in harmony with their dream-like environment, while Aquarius is constantly thinking of new ideas and methods. This pair fights for truth and innovative ideas. Both partners constantly seek out new adventures and solutions. They both benefit out of reflection. Aquarius tends to be quick to judge people who don't align with their view as well as Pisces can be incredibly caring, even for those who aren't good enough.

Aquarius and Pisces are excellent companions. There aren't many problems but occasionally Aquarius is too intelligent and distant for Pisces and Pisces could be too self-sacrificing and insecure for Aquarian preferences. Sometimes, different responses to an event could cause them to be at odds. Aquarius tends to be quick to dismiss people who aren't in line with their view, while Pisces tends to tackle everyone's problems as the chameleon. They can have disagreements, but they can easily forgive and forget.

Aquarius is and is ruled by Planets Uranus as well as Saturn and Pisces is the planet of Jupiter as well as Neptune. Uranus is a proponent of iconoclastic concepts and innovative methods. Saturn provides these friends with the confidence to implement these ideas, and also the capacity to arrange the details that can animate their lives. Jupiter is all about learning, philosophy, and understanding the world. Neptune is focused on spirituality, which is why Pisces loves to fully comprehend the new and interesting things. If Aquarius discovers some new concept and frequently do Pisces will be eager to grasp it at an intuitive perspective. The two friends have a wealth of mental and emotional sources.

Aquarius is known as an air Sign It is also a Water Sign. Pisces is a water Sign. The two are motivated by emotion and thought and vice versa. There's always a lot happening, and it's an extremely flexible and dynamic relationship. If it's going well, it's great, but when communication is poor, it is poor. Pisces prefers to be in the middle of the place where Aquarius is where action and intelligence are at the forefront and Aquarius can gain how to be a socially acceptable person and warm from the stoic Pisces. Pisces and Aquarian acquaintances work well together. While they may not agree but their disagreements aren't lasting long. Conflicts could arise as a result of Pisces need for help and Aquarius preferring ideas over emotions.

Aquarius is an Fixed Sign, while Pisces is a mutable sign. Aquarius is the one who initiates ideas and Pisces accepts these ideas so long as they have a an active role in creating it into reality. When the two spend time working together to make things happen and they don't have to debate who will get responsibility for the achievements or experiences. Both of them are better at beginning things than ending them. If Aquarius is bored by something, Pisces will soon follow the same pattern and leave the scene.

The greatest benefit of a friendship between Aquarius and Pisces is their shared passion for learning and acceptance of modern and contemporary ideas. They're well-matched in their energy, enthusiasm and desire to have a true and genuine connection. Their common interests and similar personalities make for a wholesome and rewarding friendship.

Chapter 10: The Big Picture

General stuff

Remember that the traits of an Aquarius could vary a lot based on the place in which she was born and also a broad array of other astrological variables. However, for the moment, we'll remain with the basics. Be careful not to be quick to make assumptions when you first meet her. Let her shine. Meet the person behind the sign.

Pros and pros and

Pros

* Sparkling
* Friendly
* Absurd
* Outgoing
* Kind
* Understanding
* Independent
* Creative
* Curious

Original

* Do not be afraid to begin over
* Enthusiastic
* Helpful

* An Erotic explorer

Cons

* Emotionally detached
* Restless
* Undecided about the love of your life
* Self-centred
* A slow starter that is erotically
* He ignores her feelings
* Naive
* The tendency to drift
* Undecisive
* Unsecure
* Not sensitive to the feelings of others.
* Not practical
* Self-pitying
* Instinctively ignorant

Romantic vibes

"Miss Aquarius," the passionate and feminine companion

The essence of

The "friend-zone. Everything begins with friendship and friendship will last even if things get slightly closer and more romantic. The problem is transitioning between friendship and romance. If you aren't able to entice her into a romantic relationship then you'll be in the "friends" zone.

Independent. The woman is an autonomous spouse and does not mind her personal passions.

Absentminded. There are always things going through her head and she may seem disoriented and emotional at times. This is not her intent to hide her feelings, she believes that her partner does.

A mind-reader is not a thing. She might not be aware of the needs of her partner's emotions in the event that he does not tell her. Her emotional antennas aren't very well-tuned.

Be a part of her energy. She's positive and radiant and is able to approach relationships with enthusiasm, provided her partner is also optimistic. A man who is slow and boring can drain her of enthusiasm and cause her to miserable.

Time for quality time. She is a lover of having friends around her, but she is a fan of intimacy, both physical and mental with her significant other.

Tips: How to show your love for someone else

Invite her to a party or an event that is related to something that she is attracted to. You need to feel emotionally connected to her companion, so this could be a great starting point.

Erotic vibrations

Miss Aquarius A: The energetic and kind-hearted lover

The essence:

Gentle in her ways. There's nothing threatening about her. She may be assertive but never overly aggressive.

Understanding. She is extremely proud of making her partner happy. To do this she is extremely patient. When things aren't going as smoothly she will patiently awaken her companion until he's ready to move.

An erotic adventurer. Her passion for adventure is paramount to her and she is always looking for different ways of interpreting traditional themes to keep her sex experience interesting and fresh.

Sensual firework. While she might appear as a slow walker however, there's nothing slow about her. She'll prove to be a bonfire full of pleasures sexual.

Erotic spice. When she's in a good mood, she's keen to test new concepts. She's extremely creative and has the unique ability to bring a smile to any situation with an erotic zing.

Intimacy is a huge factor for her. Gentle touches and gentle caresses are the most important thing she needs to feel a sense of pleasure.

The pleasure of sharing. Being able to please her partner is just the same as being happy herself , sometimes even more. Being attentive to the needs of her companion is a natural trait for her.

TIP: How to display an interest in erotica
Create your own ideas about it. Ask her questions about exotic sensuality like tantric sex and whether it's an unpopular trend or actually something that could increase your sensual pleasure.

Aquarius arousal meter
From Zero from 0 to... From 0 to 100... or more. She is a lover of exploring sexuality gradually. She's a little impulsive but she also is patient.

Compatibility Quiz
Are you hitting your head on the wall? Or is she letting out your best potential? Do you get her offended or draw out the best of her? Do you feel like she is causing you to throw your arms up in the air to express your frustration or do you feel energized and complete within her presence? Test it to discover the answer.

Question 1
Have you ever thought about the idea of trying out erotic activities that are unusual?
A. Yes, I have fantasies but I usually let them be.
B. No I prefer to stay secure and comfortable!
C. Yes, several times. I've even attempted tantric sex. It's extremely satisfying.

Question 2

While having a sex break the partner suddenly ceases her activities and begins telling you about an exciting thing that she experienced earlier in the day. Well..?

A. I think this is my cue to fall asleep.

B. I'm sure I'll not think about the sexual aspect. My girlfriend is engaging and entertaining, and I enjoy watching her.

C. Typical. My reaction was to giggle and then hit her on the head with the pillow.

3.

It's a hot morning and you wake up feeling extremely hot. What do you do when your spouse doesn't pay attention to you and starts talking to them about plans to spend the next day?

A. No big deal. I'm pretty excited myself.

B. I'd lay the blanket on my head, and then'sort things out on my own.

C. My first response would be: Yes however, make sure you dress in a sexy outfit the moment you return...

Question 4.

Your toolbox isn't working as it should one night. What would you like your partner do?

A. She is focusing on herself and keeping an my attention.
B. Nothing. Let me be alone.
C. Show love and play with my tools for a to see what happens.

5.

Do you find it surprising when your lover asked you to talk about your sexual past?

A. Not at all. Sharing your sexual experiences is a crucial aspect of establishing an appropriate sexual life.
B. Maybe. I'm sure it would cause me to be shy.
C. My prior sexual encounters aren't anyone's business.

Question 6.

Are you flexible?

A. It's not really.
B. Yes. I am having a blast everywhere I go.
C. Yes But, it's not always.

Question 7.

Do you find it difficult to accept that your partner doesn't appear especially dependent on you?

A. Not at all. Actually this makes me feel happy. I'm happy she's an independent woman.

B. Yes. this is my main concern. I'm quite jealous.

C. I'm having mixed feelings. I'm happy she's independent and independent, but I'd like to be part of her life and be a part of her life.

Question 8.

Do you often feel like the person you love is interested more in your thoughts than in your body?

A. Yes, and even though I realize that I shouldn't take it as an compliment, it does cause me to feel angry.

B. Body and mind? They're one thing, isn't it?

C. She loves me. This is enough for me.

Question 9.

Have you ever been so absorbed in the game that you didn't think to mention an extra-gasmass?

A. No! That's impossible.

B. A. Once or twice, but only when I'm in a good mood.

C. Many times. Sexual pleasure is more than only orgasms.

Question 10.

Are you easily impulsive?

A. Yes, very. My friends say I'm just a bit sometimes impulsive.

B. No, I am a firm believer in the power of planning!

C. Sometimes it happens, when I'm not.

Score:

Question 1

A 5 points

B 1 point

C 10 points

Question 2

A 1 point

B 10 points

C 5 points

Question 3

A 10 points

B 5 points

C 1 point

Question 4

A 5 points

B 1 point

C 10 points

Question 5
A 10 points
B 5 points
C 1 point
Question 6
A 1 point
B 10 points
C 5 points
Question 7
A 10 points
B 1 point
C 5 points
Question 8
A 5 points
B 10 points
C 1 point
Question 9
A 1 point
B 5 points
C 10 points
Question 10
A 10 points
B 1 point
C 5 points
75 - 100

Do you have the time to get out and meet your acquaintances? There is a good chance that the two of you are enjoying the company of each other such that you want to become absorbed in your shared adventures, ideas, and any other thing that could broaden your perspectives. You've found an energy that is new to you that you can apply to every situation, including sexual. Every day is a new adventure to discover. Stay with her and you'll never get bored.

51 - 74

Be flexible and open You'll not encounter any bumps in the road. She's a wild woman and this is something that inspires your more so than it annoys you. It's a great feeling to have someone around who gets up each day and is awed by the world. She inspires you to think and feel alive. As a result, you provide her the courage and the confidence she seeks regardless of whether she's willing to acknowledge it. Sensuality brings you closer and lets you communicate on multiple levels. Maintain this connection.

26 - 50

Are you feeling breathless? Take a moment and reflect. Are you drawn to the adventure, or do you feel drawn by the girl? She's impulsive and draws your energy to the surface However, do you feel alive or tired? To make maximum enjoyment from this relationship, you have to determine if she meets your needs at the core. If she does not and it doesn't, it's not going to last for long. In the event that she is, it may be beneficial to keep in touch to avoid confusion. Try to be more flexible and flexible. This will help her feel more comfortable. If you'd like to make a change, inform her. She's not a mind-reader.

10 - 25

It could be much better. What is the reason you are stuck? have you ever attempted to catch a butterfly without damaging its wings? When you are looking to discuss something important or have an intimate moment, she's usually wandering around by herself. This isn't the foundation of your ideal relationship.

Although she's fun and fascinating but there's something lacking. It's a rush and superficial. There is no time for level of. If you're not on the same page it's difficult to get her to understand and adapt. Happiness and fulfillment await elsewhere for you both.

Conclusion

Thank you for reading! the Aquarian's aren't like other people They are aware of the sufferings of the world but not to them. They are prepared for every kind of challenge in life , to reach highest levels. They are born leaders to manage large groups and organizations. Numerous astrologers, preachers, CEO's of companies are associated with this sign. They're the least efficient when it comes to doing things for themselves.

Thank you! !

www.ingramcontent.com/pod-product-compliance
Lightning Source LLC
Chambersburg PA
CBHW050400120526
44590CB00015B/1767